TExES

Middle School Sample Test Kit:

THEA
Pedagogy & Professional Responsibilities EC-12
Generalist 4-8

Teacher Certification Exam

By: Sharon Wynne, M.S.

XAMonline, INC.

Boston

To obtain permission(s) to use the material from this work for any purpose including workshops or seminars, please submit a written request to:

XAMonline, Inc.
25 First Street, Suite 106
Cambridge, MA 02141
Toll Free: 1-800-509-4128
Email: info@xamonline.com
Web: www.xamonline.com
Fax: 1-617-583-5552

Library of Congress Cataloging-in-Publication Data

Wynne, Sharon A.
TExES Middle School Sample Test Kit: THEA, PPR EC-12, Generalist 4-8:
Teacher Certification / Sharon A. Wynne. -1st ed.
ISBN: 978-1-60787-307-5
1. TExES Pedagogy and Professional Responsibilities EC-12 Practice Test 1
2. Study Guides   3. TExES   4. Teachers' Certification & Licensure
5. Careers

Disclaimer:
The opinions expressed in this publication are the sole works of XAMonline and were created independently from the National Education Association, Educational Testing Service, or any State Department of Education, National Evaluation Systems or other testing affiliates.

Between the time of publication and printing, state specific standards as well as testing formats and website information may change that is not included in part or in whole within this product. Sample test questions are developed by XAMonline and reflect similar content as on real tests; however, they are not former tests. XAMonline assembles content that aligns with state standards but makes no claims nor guarantees teacher candidates a passing score. Numerical scores are determined by testing companies such as NES or ETS and then are compared with individual state standards. A passing score varies from state to state.

Printed in the United States of America   œ-1
TExES Middle School Sample Test Kit: THEA, PPR EC-12, Generalist 4-8
ISBN: 978-1-60787-307-5

TABLE OF CONTENTS

THEA TEXAS HIGHER EDUCATION ASSESSMENT

READING SAMPLE TEST

Read the following paragraph, and answer the questions that follow.

This writer has often been asked to tutor hospitalized children with cystic fibrosis. While undergoing all the precautionary measures to see these children (i.e., scrubbing thoroughly and donning sterilized protective gear—for the children's protection), she has often wondered why their parents subject these children to the pressures of schooling and trying to catch up on what they have missed because of hospitalization, a normal part of cystic fibrosis patients' lives. These children undergo so many tortuous treatments a day that it seems cruel to expect them to learn as normal children do, especially with their life expectancies as short as they are.

1. **What is meant by the word "precautionary" in the second sentence?**
   (Easy)

   A. Careful
   B. Protective
   C. Medical
   D. Sterilizing

2. **What is the main idea of this passage?**
   (Average)

   A. There is a lot of preparation involved in visiting a patient of cystic fibrosis.
   B. Children with cystic fibrosis are incapable of living normal lives.
   C. Certain concessions should be made for children with cystic fibrosis.
   D. Children with cystic fibrosis die young.

3. **What is the author's purpose?**
   (Average)

   A. To inform
   B. To entertain
   C. To describe
   D. To narrate

4. **What is the author's tone?**
   (Rigorous)

   A. Sympathetic
   B. Cruel
   C. Disbelieving
   D. Cheerful

5. **What type of organizational pattern is the author using?**
   (Rigorous)

   A. Classification
   B. Explanation
   C. Compare and contrast
   D. Cause and effect

6. How is the author so familiar with the procedures used when visiting a child with cystic fibrosis?
(Easy)

   A. She has read about it.
   B. She works in a hospital.
   C. She is the parent of one.
   D. She often tutors them.

7. What kind of relationship is found within the last sentence that starts with "These children undergo..." and ends with "...as short as they are"?
(Rigorous)

   A. Addition
   B. Explanation
   C. Generalization
   D. Classification

8. Does the author present an argument that is valid or invalid concerning the schooling of children with cystic fibrosis?
(Easy)

   A. Valid
   B. Invalid

9. The author states that it is "cruel" to expect children with cystic fibrosis to learn as "normal" children do. Is this a fact or an opinion?
(Easy)

   A. Fact
   B. Opinion

10. Is there evidence of bias in this paragraph?
(Rigorous)

    A. Yes
    B. No

Read the following passage, and answer the questions that follow.

Disciplinary practices have been found to affect diverse areas of child development such as moral values, obedience to authority, and performance at school. Even though the dictionary has a specific definition for the word "discipline," it is still open to interpretation by people of different cultures.

There are four types of disciplinary styles: assertion of power, withdrawal of love, reasoning, and permissiveness. Assertion of power involves the use of force to discourage unwanted behavior. Withdrawal of love involves making the love of a parent conditional on children's good behavior. Reasoning involves persuading children to behave one way rather than another. Permissiveness involves allowing children to do as they please and face the consequences of their actions.

11. **What is the meaning of the word "diverse" in the first sentence?**
   (Average)

   A. Many
   B. Related to children
   C. Disciplinary
   D. More

12. **What is the main idea of this passage?**
   (Easy)

   A. Different people have different ideas of what discipline is.
   B. Permissiveness is the most widely used disciplinary style.
   C. Most people agree on their definition of discipline.
   D. There are four disciplinary styles.

13. **Name the four types of disciplinary styles.**
   (Easy)

   A. Reasoning, power assertion, morality, and permissiveness
   B. Morality, reasoning, permissiveness, and withdrawal of love
   C. Withdrawal of love, permissiveness, assertion of power, and reasoning
   D. Permissiveness, morality, reasoning, and power assertion

14. **What does the technique of reasoning involve?**
   (Average)

   A. Persuading children to behave in a certain way
   B. Allowing a child to do as he or she pleases
   C. Using force to discourage unwanted behavior
   D. Making love conditional on good behavior

15. **What organizational structure is used in the first sentence of the second paragraph?**
(Rigorous)

   A. Addition
   B. Explanation
   C. Definition
   D. Simple listing

16. **What is the author's purpose in writing this?**
(Average)

   A. To describe
   B. To narrate
   C. To entertain
   D. To inform

17. **What is the author's tone?**
(Rigorous)

   A. Disbelieving
   B. Angry
   C. Informative
   D. Optimistic

18. **What is the overall organizational pattern of this passage?**
(Rigorous)

   A. Generalization
   B. Cause and effect
   C. Addition
   D. Summary

19. **From reading this passage we can conclude that**
(Average)

   A. The author is a teacher.
   B. The author has many children.
   C. The author has written a book about discipline.
   D. The author has done a lot of research on discipline.

20. **The author states that "assertion of power involves the use of force to discourage unwanted behavior." Is this a fact or an opinion?**
(Average)

   A. Fact
   B. Opinion

21. **Is this passage biased?**
(Rigorous)

   A. Yes
   B. No

Read the following passage, and answer the questions that follow.

One of the most difficult problems plaguing American education is the assessment of teachers. No one denies that teachers ought to be answerable for what they do, but what exactly does that mean? *The Oxford American Dictionary* defines accountability as the obligation to give a reckoning or explanation for one's actions.

Do students have to learn, for teaching to have taken place? Historically, teaching has not been defined in this restrictive manner; teachers were thought to be responsible for the quantity and quality of material covered and for the way in which it was presented. However, some definitions of teaching now imply that students must learn in order for teaching to have taken place.

As a teacher who tries my best to keep current on all the latest teaching strategies, I believe that those teachers who do not bother to read an educational journal every once in a while should be kept under close watch. There are many teachers out there who have been teaching for decades and refuse to change their ways, although research has proven that their methods are outdated and ineffective. There is no place in the profession of teaching for these types of individuals. It is time that the American educational system clean house, for the sake of our children.

22. **What is the meaning of the word "reckoning" in the third sentence?**
(Easy)

A. Thought
B. Answer
C. Obligation
D. Explanation

23. **What is meant by the word "plaguing" in the first sentence?**
(Average)

A. Causing problems
B. Causing illness
C. Causing anger
D. Causing failure

24. **Where does the author get her definition of "accountability?"**
(Average)

A. *Webster's Dictionary*
B. *Encyclopedia Britannica*
C. *Oxford Dictionary*
D. *World Book Encyclopedia*

25. **What is the main idea of the passage?**
(Average)

A. Teachers should not be answerable for what they do.
B. Teachers who do not do their job should be fired.
C. The author is a good teacher.
D. Assessment of teachers is a serious problem in society today.

26. **The author states that teacher assessment is a problem for**
    (Average)

    A. Elementary schools
    B. Secondary schools
    C. American education
    D. Families

27. **What is the author's purpose in writing this?**
    (Average)

    A. To entertain
    B. To narrate
    C. To describe
    D. To persuade

28. **The author's tone is one of**
    (Rigorous)

    A. Disbelief
    B. Excitement
    C. Support
    D. Concern

29. **Is there evidence of bias in this passage?**
    (Rigorous)

    A. Yes
    B. No

30. **What is the organizational pattern of the second paragraph?**
    (Rigorous)

    A. Cause and effect
    B. Classification
    C. Addition
    D. Explanation

31. **From the passage, one can infer that**
    (Average)

    A. The author considers himself or herself to be a good teacher.
    B. Poor teachers should be fired.
    C. Students have to learn for teaching to take place.
    D. The author will be fired.

32. **Is this a valid argument?**
    (Easy)

    A. Yes
    B. No

33. **Teachers who do not keep current on educational trends should be fired. Is this a fact or an opinion?**
    (Easy)

    A. Fact
    B. Opinion

34. **What is the best summary for the passage?**
    (Average)

    A. Teachers need to be more accountable.
    B. Today's teachers must be responsible for student learning.
    C. Older teachers have no place in the classroom.
    D. Teachers are responsible for the quantity they teach, not the quality.

Read the following paragraph, and answer the questions that follow.
Mr. Smith gave instructions for the painting to be hung on the wall. And then it leaped forth before his eyes: the little cottages on the river, the white clouds floating over the valley, and the green of the towering mountain ranges which were seen in the distance. The painting was so vivid that it seemed almost real. Mr. Smith was now absolutely certain that the painting had been worth the money.

35. **What is the meaning of the word "vivid" in the third sentence?**
(Easy)

   A. Lifelike
   B. Dark
   C. Expensive
   D. Big

36. **What does the author mean by the expression "it leaped forth before his eyes"?**
(Average)

   A. The painting fell off the wall.
   B. The painting appeared so real it was almost three-dimensional.
   C. The painting struck Mr. Smith in the face.
   D. Mr. Smith was hallucinating.

37. **What is the main idea of this passage?**
(Average)

   A. The painting that Mr. Smith purchased is expensive.
   B. Mr. Smith purchased a painting.
   C. Mr. Smith was pleased with the quality of the painting he had purchased.
   D. The painting depicted cottages and valleys.

38. **The author's purpose is to**
(Average)

   A. Inform
   B. Entertain
   C. Persuade
   D. Narrate

39. **From the last sentence, one can infer that**
(Rigorous)

   A. The painting was expensive.
   B. The painting was cheap.
   C. Mr. Smith was considering purchasing the painting.
   D. Mr. Smith thought the painting was too expensive and decided not to purchase it.

40. **Is this passage biased?**
(Rigorous)

   A. Yes
   B. No

Answer Key

1.	B		21.	B
2.	C		22.	D
3.	C		23.	A
4.	A		24.	C
5.	B		25.	D
6.	D		26.	C
7.	B		27.	D
8.	B		28.	D
9.	B		29.	A
10.	A		30.	D
11.	A		31.	A
12.	A		32.	B
13.	C		33.	B
14.	A		34.	B
15.	D		35.	A
16.	D		36.	B
17.	C		37.	C
18.	C		38.	D
19.	D		39.	A
20.	A		40.	B

Rigor Table

Easy
1, 6, 8, 9, 12, 13, 22, 32, 33, 35

Average
2, 3, 11, 14, 16, 19, 20, 23, 24, 25, 26, 27, 31, 34, 36, 37, 38

Rigorous
4, 5, 7, 10, 15, 17, 18, 21, 28, 29, 30, 39, 40

READING SAMPLE TEST WITH RATIONALES

Read the following paragraph, and answer the questions that follow.
This writer has often been asked to tutor hospitalized children with cystic fibrosis. While undergoing all the precautionary measures to see these children (i.e., scrubbing thoroughly and donning sterilized protective gear—for the children's protection), she has often wondered why their parents subject these children to the pressures of schooling and trying to catch up on what they have missed because of hospitalization, a normal part of cystic fibrosis patients' lives. These children undergo so many tortuous treatments a day that it seems cruel to expect them to learn as normal children do, especially with their life expectancies as short as they are.

1. **What is meant by the word "precautionary" in the second sentence? (Easy)**

   A. Careful
   B. Protective
   C. Medical
   D. Sterilizing

Answer: B. Protective
The writer uses expressions such as "protective gear" and "child's protection" to emphasize this.

2. **What is the main idea of this passage? (Average)**

   A. There is a lot of preparation involved in visiting a patient of cystic fibrosis.
   B. Children with cystic fibrosis are incapable of living normal lives.
   C. Certain concessions should be made for children with cystic fibrosis.
   D. Children with cystic fibrosis die young.

Answer: C. Certain concessions should be made for children with cystic fibrosis
The author states that she wonders "why parents subject these children to the pressures of schooling," and that "it seems cruel to expect them to learn as normal children do." In making these statements, she appears to be expressing the belief that these children should not have to do what "normal" children do. They have enough to deal with—their illness itself.

3. **What is the author's purpose?**
   (Average)

   A. To inform
   B. To entertain
   C. To describe
   D. To narrate

Answer: C. To describe
The author is simply describing her experience in working with children with cystic fibrosis.

4. **What is the author's tone?**
   (Rigorous)

   A. Sympathetic
   B. Cruel
   C. Disbelieving
   D. Cheerful

Answer: A. Sympathetic
The author states that "it seems cruel to expect them to learn as normal children do," thereby indicating that she feels sorry for them.

5. **What type of organizational pattern is the author using?**
   (Rigorous)

   A. Classification
   B. Explanation
   C. Compare and contrast
   D. Cause and effect

Answer: B. Explanation
The author mentions tutoring children with cystic fibrosis in her opening sentence and goes on to "explain" some of these issues that are involved with her job.

6.   **How is the author so familiar with the procedures used when visiting a child with cystic fibrosis?**
      (Easy)

      A. She has read about it.
      B. She works in a hospital.
      C. She is the parent of one.
      D. She often tutors them.

Answer: D. She often tutors them.
The writer states this fact in the opening sentence.

7.   **What kind of relationship is found within the last sentence that starts with "These children undergo..." and ends with "...as short as they are"?**
      (Rigorous)

      A. Addition
      B. Explanation
      C. Generalization
      D. Classification

Answer: B. Explanation
In mentioning that their life expectancies are short, she is explaining by giving one reason why it is cruel to expect them to learn as normal children do.

8.   **Does the author present an argument that is valid or invalid concerning the schooling of children with cystic fibrosis?**
      (Easy)

      A. Valid
      B. Invalid

Answer: B. Invalid
Even though to most readers, the writer's argument makes good sense, it is biased and lacks real evidence.

9. **The author states that it is "cruel" to expect children with cystic fibrosis to learn as "normal" children do. Is this a fact or an opinion?** *(Easy)*

   A. Fact
   B. Opinion

Answer: B. Opinion
The fact that she states that it "seems" cruel indicates that there is no evidence to support this belief.

10. **Is there evidence of bias in this paragraph?** *(Rigorous)*

   A. Yes
   B. No

Answer: A. Yes
The writer clearly feels sorry for these children and gears her writing in that direction.

Read the following passage, and answer the questions that follow.
Disciplinary practices have been found to affect diverse areas of child development such as moral values, obedience to authority, and performance at school. Even though the dictionary has a specific definition for the word "discipline," it is still open to interpretation by people of different cultures.

There are four types of disciplinary styles: assertion of power, withdrawal of love, reasoning, and permissiveness. Assertion of power involves the use of force to discourage unwanted behavior. Withdrawal of love involves making the love of a parent conditional on children's good behavior. Reasoning involves persuading children to behave one way rather than another. Permissiveness involves allowing children to do as they please and face the consequences of their actions.

11. **What is the meaning of the word "diverse" in the first sentence?** *(Average)*

   A. Many
   B. Related to children
   C. Disciplinary
   D. More

Answer: A. Many
Any of the other choices would be redundant in this sentence.

12. **What is the main idea of this passage?**
   (Easy)

    A. Different people have different ideas of what discipline is.
    B. Permissiveness is the most widely used disciplinary style.
    C. Most people agree on their definition of discipline.
    D. There are four disciplinary styles.

Answer: A. Different people have different ideas of what discipline is.
Choice C is not true; the opposite is stated in the passage. Choice B could be true, but we have no evidence of this. Choice D is just one of the many facts listed in the passage.

13. **Name the four types of disciplinary styles.**
   (Easy)

    A. Reasoning, power assertion, morality, and permissiveness
    B. Morality, reasoning, permissiveness, and withdrawal of love
    C. Withdrawal of love, permissiveness, assertion of power, and reasoning
    D. Permissiveness, morality, reasoning, and power assertion

Answer: C. Withdrawal of love, permissiveness, assertion of power, and reasoning
This is directly stated in the second paragraph.

14. **What does the technique of reasoning involve?**
   (Average)

    A. Persuading children to behave in a certain way
    B. Allowing a child to do as he or she pleases
    C. Using force to discourage unwanted behavior
    D. Making love conditional on good behavior

Answer: A. Persuading children to behave in a certain way
This fact is directly stated in the second paragraph.

15. **What organizational structure is used in the first sentence of the second paragraph?**
    (Rigorous)

    A. Addition
    B. Explanation
    C. Definition
    D. Simple listing

Answer: D. Simple listing
The author simply states the types of disciplinary styles.

16. **What is the author's purpose in writing this?**
    (Average)

    A. To describe
    B. To narrate
    C. To entertain
    D. To inform

Answer: D. To inform
The author is providing the reader with information about disciplinary practices.

17. **What is the author's tone?**
    (Rigorous)

    A. Disbelieving
    B. Angry
    C. Informative
    D. Optimistic

Answer: C. Informative
The author appears to simply be stating the facts.

18. **What is the overall organizational pattern of this passage?**
    (Rigorous)

    A. Generalization
    B. Cause and effect
    C. Addition
    D. Summary

Answer: C. Addition
The author has taken a subject, in this case discipline, and developed it point by point.

19. **From reading this passage we can conclude that**
    (Average)

    A. The author is a teacher.
    B. The author has many children.
    C. The author has written a book about discipline.
    D. The author has done a lot of research on discipline.

Answer: D. The author has done a lot of research on discipline.
Given all the facts mentioned in the passage, this is the only inference one can make.

20. **The author states that "assertion of power involves the use of force to discourage unwanted behavior." Is this a fact or an opinion?**
    (Average)

    A. Fact
    B. Opinion

Answer: A. Fact
The author appears to have done extensive research on this subject.

21. **Is this passage biased?**
    (Rigorous)

    A. Yes
    B. No

Answer: B. No
If the reader were so inclined, he could research discipline and find this information.

Read the following passage, and answer the questions that follow.

One of the most difficult problems plaguing American education is the assessment of teachers. No one denies that teachers ought to be answerable for what they do, but what exactly does that mean? *The Oxford American Dictionary* defines accountability as the obligation to give a reckoning or explanation for one's actions.

Do students have to learn, for teaching to have taken place? Historically, teaching has not been defined in this restrictive manner; teachers were thought to be responsible for the quantity and quality of material covered and for the way in which it was presented. However, some definitions of teaching now imply that students must learn in order for teaching to have taken place.

As a teacher who tries my best to keep current on all the latest teaching strategies, I believe that those teachers who do not bother to read an educational journal every once in a while should be kept under close watch. There are many teachers out there who have been teaching for decades and refuse to change their ways, although research has proven that their methods are outdated and ineffective. There is no place in the profession of teaching for these types of individuals. It is time that the American educational system clean house, for the sake of our children.

22. **What is the meaning of the word "reckoning" in the third sentence?** *(Easy)*

    A. Thought
    B. Answer
    C. Obligation
    D. Explanation

Answer: D. Explanation
The meaning of this word is directly stated in the same sentence.

23. **What is meant by the word "plaguing" in the first sentence?** *(Average)*

    A. Causing problems
    B. Causing illness
    C. Causing anger
    D. Causing failure

Answer: A. Causing problems
The first paragraph makes this definition clear.

24. **Where does the author get her definition of "accountability?"**
(Average)

   A. _Webster's Dictionary_
   B. _Encyclopedia Britannica_
   C. _Oxford Dictionary_
   D. _World Book Encyclopedia_

Answer: C. _Oxford Dictionary_
This is directly stated in the third sentence of the first paragraph.

25. **What is the main idea of the passage?**
(Average)

   A. Teachers should not be answerable for what they do.
   B. Teachers who do not do their job should be fired.
   C. The author is a good teacher.
   D. Assessment of teachers is a serious problem in society today.

Answer: D. Assessment of teachers is a serious problem in society today.
Most of the passage is dedicated to elaborating on why teacher assessment is such a problem.

26. **The author states that teacher assessment is a problem for**
(Average)

   A. Elementary schools
   B. Secondary schools
   C. American education
   D. Families

Answer: C. American education
This fact is directly stated in the first paragraph.

27. **What is the author's purpose in writing this?**
(Average)

   A. To entertain
   B. To narrate
   C. To describe
   D. To persuade

Answer: D. To persuade
The author does some describing, but the majority of her statements seemed geared towards convincing the reader that teachers who are lazy or who do not keep current should be fired.

28. **The author's tone is one of**
(Rigorous)

   A. Disbelief
   B. Excitement
   C. Support
   D. Concern

Answer: D. Concern
The author appears concerned with the future of education.

29. **Is there evidence of bias in this passage?**
(Rigorous)

   A. Yes
   B. No

Answer: A. Yes
The entire third paragraph is the author's opinion on the matter.

30. **What is the organizational pattern of the second paragraph?**
(Rigorous)

   A. Cause and effect
   B. Classification
   C. Addition
   D. Explanation

Answer: D. Explanation
The author further explains what she meant by "...what exactly does that mean?" in the first paragraph.

31. **From the passage, one can infer that**
(Average)

   A. The author considers himself or herself to be a good teacher.
   B. Poor teachers should be fired.
   C. Students have to learn for teaching to take place.
   D. The author will be fired.

Answer: A. The author considers himself or herself to be a good teacher.
The first sentence of the third paragraph alludes to this.

32. **Is this a valid argument?**
   (Easy)

   A. Yes
   B. No

Answer: B. No
In the third paragraph, the author appears to be resentful of lazy teachers.

33. **Teachers who do not keep current on educational trends should be fired. Is this a fact or an opinion?**
   (Easy)

   A. Fact
   B. Opinion

Answer: B. Opinion
There may be those who feel they can be good teachers by using old methods.

34. **What is the best summary for the passage?**
   (Average)

   A. Teachers need to be more accountable.
   B. Today's teachers must be responsible for student learning.
   C. Older teachers have no place in the classroom.
   D. Teachers are responsible for the quantity they teach, not the quality.

Answer: B. Today's teachers must be responsible for student learning.
The one idea that applies to the whole passage is Choice B.

Read the following paragraph, and answer the questions that follow.
Mr. Smith gave instructions for the painting to be hung on the wall. And then it leaped forth before his eyes: the little cottages on the river, the white clouds floating over the valley, and the green of the towering mountain ranges which were seen in the distance. The painting was so vivid that it seemed almost real. Mr. Smith was now absolutely certain that the painting had been worth the money.

35. **What is the meaning of the word "vivid" in the third sentence?**
(Easy)

   A. Lifelike
   B. Dark
   C. Expensive
   D. Big

Answer: A. Lifelike
This is reinforced by the second half of the same sentence.

36. **What does the author mean by the expression "it leaped forth before his eyes"?**
(Average)

   A. The painting fell off the wall.
   B. The painting appeared so real it was almost three-dimensional.
   C. The painting struck Mr. Smith in the face.
   D. Mr. Smith was hallucinating.

Answer: B. The painting appeared so real it was almost three-dimensional
This is almost directly stated in the third sentence.

37. **What is the main idea of this passage?**
(Average)

   A. The painting that Mr. Smith purchased is expensive.
   B. Mr. Smith purchased a painting.
   C. Mr. Smith was pleased with the quality of the painting he had purchased.
   D. The painting depicted cottages and valleys.

Answer: C. Mr. Smith was pleased with the quality of the painting he had purchased.
Every sentence in the paragraph alludes to this fact.

38. **The author's purpose is to**
(Average)

  A. Inform
  B. Entertain
  C. Persuade
  D. Narrate

Answer: D. Narrate
The author is simply narrating or telling the story of Mr. Smith and his painting.

39. **From the last sentence, one can infer that**
(Rigorous)

  A. The painting was expensive.
  B. The painting was cheap.
  C. Mr. Smith was considering purchasing the painting.
  D. Mr. Smith thought the painting was too expensive and decided not to purchase it.

Answer: A. The painting was expensive.
Choice B is incorrect because, had the painting been cheap, chances are that Mr. Smith would not have considered his purchase. Choices C and D are ruled out by the fact that the painting had already been purchased. The author makes this clear when she says, "...the painting had been worth the money."

40. **Is this passage biased?**
(Rigorous)

  A. Yes
  B. No

Answer: B. No
The author appears merely to be telling what happened when Mr. Smith had his new painting hung on the wall.

MATHEMATICS SAMPLE TEST

1. $\left(\dfrac{-4}{9}\right) + \left(\dfrac{-7}{10}\right) =$

   (Rigorous)

   A. $\dfrac{23}{90}$

   B. $\dfrac{-23}{90}$

   C. $\dfrac{103}{90}$

   D. $\dfrac{-103}{90}$

2. $0.74 =$

   (Easy)

   A. $\dfrac{74}{100}$

   B. 7.4%

   C. $\dfrac{33}{50}$

   D. $\dfrac{74}{10}$

3. $-9\dfrac{1}{4}$ ☐ $-8\dfrac{2}{3}$

   (Average)

   A. $=$
   B. $<$
   C. $>$
   D. $\leq$

4. **303 is what percent of 600?**
   (Average)

   A. 0.505%
   B. 5.05%
   C. 505%
   D. 50.5%

5. **An item that sells for $375 is put on sale at $120. What is the percent of decrease?**
   (Average)

   A. 25%
   B. 28%
   C. 68%
   D. 34%

6. **Two mathematics classes have a total of 410 students. The 8:00 am class has 40 more than the 10:00 am class. How many students are in the 10:00 am class?**
   (Average)

   A. 123.3
   B. 370
   C. 185
   D. 330

7. **A restaurant employs 465 people. There are 280 waiters and 185 cooks. If 168 waiters and 85 cooks receive pay raises, what percent of the waiters will receive a pay raise?**
   (Average)

   A. 36.13%
   B. 60%
   C. 60.22%
   D. 40%

8. $\dfrac{7}{9} + \dfrac{1}{3} \div \dfrac{2}{3} =$
(Average)

A. $\dfrac{5}{3}$

B. $\dfrac{3}{2}$

C. 2

D. $\dfrac{23}{18}$

9. Choose the statement that is true for all real numbers.
(Rigorous)

A. $a = 0, b \neq 0$, then $\dfrac{b}{a} =$ undefined.

B. $^-(a + (^-a)) = 2a$

C. $2(ab) = ^-(2a)b$

D. $^-a(b + 1) = ab - a$

10. The price of gas was $3.27 per gallon. Your tank holds 15 gallons of fuel. You are using two tanks a week. How much will you save weekly if the price of gas goes down to $2.30 per gallon?
(Average)

A. $26.00
B. $29.00
C. $15.00
D. $17.00

11. In a sample of 40 full-time employees at a particular company, 35 were also holding down a part-time job requiring at least 10 hours/week. If this proportion holds for the entire company of 25000 employees, how many full-time employees at this company are actually holding down a part-time job of at least 10 hours per week?
(Rigorous)

A. 714
B. 625
C. 21,875
D. 28,571

12. A sofa sells for $520. If the retailer makes a 30% profit, what was the wholesale price?
(Average)

A. $400
B. $676
C. $490
D. $364

13. A car gets 25.36 miles per gallon. The car has been driven 83,310 miles. What is a reasonable estimate for the number of gallons of gas used?
(Average)

A. 2,087 gallons
B. 3,000 gallons
C. 1,800 gallons
D. 164 gallons

14. **What unit of measurement could we use to report the distance traveled walking around a track?**
(Easy)

   A. degrees
   B. square meters
   C. kilometers
   D. cubic feet

15. **What unit of measurement would describe the spread of a forest fire in a unit time?**
(Average)

   A. 10 square yards per second
   B. 10 yards per minute
   C. 10 feet per hour
   D. 10 cubic feet per hour

16. **Express .0000456 in scientific notation.**
(Easy)

   A. $4.56 x 10^{-4}$
   B. $45.6 x 10^{-6}$
   C. $4.56 x 10^{-6}$
   D. $4.56 x 10^{-5}$

17. **A student organization is interested in determining how strong the support is among registered voters in the United States for the president's education plan. Which of the following procedures would be most appropriate for selecting a statistically unbiased sample?**
(Average)

   A. Having viewers call in to a nationally broad-cast talk show and give their opinions.
   B. Survey registered voters selected by blind drawing in the three largest states.
   C. Select regions of the country by blind drawing and then select people from the voter's registration list by blind drawing.
   D. Pass out survey forms at the front entrance of schools selected by blind drawing and ask people entering and exiting to fill them in.

18. The following chart shows the yearly average number of international tourists visiting Palm Beach for 1990-1994. How many more international tourists visited Palm Beach in 1994 than in 1991?
(Easy)

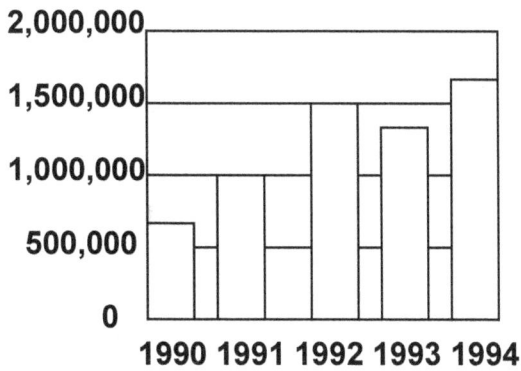

1990 1991 1992 1993 1994

A. 100,000
B. 600,000
C. 1,600,000
D. 8,000,000

19. Consider the graph of the distribution of the length of time it took individuals to complete an employment form.
(Average)

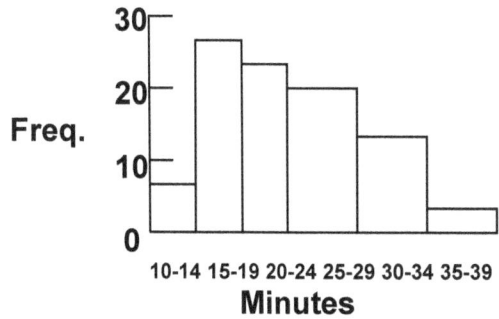

Minutes

Approximately how many individuals took less than 15 minutes to complete the employment form?

A. 35
B. 28
C. 7
D. 4

20. Which statement is true about George's budget? *(Easy)*

    A. George spends the greatest portion of his income on food.
    B. George spends twice as much on utilities as he does on his mortgage.
    C. George spends twice as much on utilities as he does on food.
    D. George spends the same amount on food and utilities as he does on mortgage.

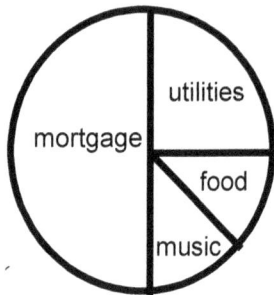

21. Corporate salaries are listed for several employees. Which is the best measure of central tendency? *(Average)*

$24,000 $24,000 $26,000
$28,000 $30,000 $120,000

    A. Mean
    B. Median
    C. Mode
    D. No difference

22. Compute the median for the following data set: *(Easy)*

{12, 19, 13, 16, 17, 14}

    A. 14.5
    B. 15.17
    C. 15
    D. 16

23. State the domain of the function $f(x) = \dfrac{3x-6}{x^2-25}$ *(Rigorous)*

    A. $x \neq 2$
    B. $x \neq 5, -5$
    C. $x \neq 2, -2$
    D. $x \neq 5$

24. Which graph represents the equation of $y = x^2 + 3x$? *(Rigorous)*

    A.   B.

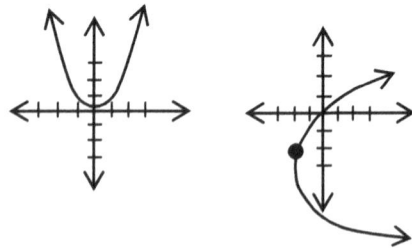

    C.   D.

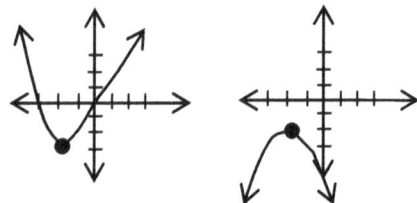

25. Choose the equation that is equivalent to the following: *(Rigorous)*

$$\frac{3x}{5} - 5 = 5x$$

A. $3x - 25 = 25x$

B. $x - \frac{25}{3} = 25x$

C. $6x - 50 = 75x$

D. $x + 25 = 25x$

26. If $4x - (3 - x) = 7(x - 3) + 10$, then *(Rigorous)*

A. $x = 8$
B. $x = -8$
C. $x = 4$
D. $x = -4$

27. Solve for x.
$$3x - \frac{2}{3} = \frac{5x}{2} + 2$$
(Rigorous)

A. $5\frac{1}{3}$

B. $\frac{17}{3}$

C. 2

D. $\frac{16}{2}$

28. Given the formula *d =rt*, (where *d* = distance, *r* =rate, and *t* =time), calculate the time required for a vehicle to travel 585 miles at a rate of 65 miles per hour. *(Average)*

A. 8.5 hours
B. 6.5 hours
C. 9.5 hours
D. 9 hours

29. Solve the system of equations for x, y and z. *(Rigorous)*

$$3x + 2y - z = 0$$
$$2x + 5y = 8z$$
$$x + 3y + 2z = 7$$

A. $(-1, \ 2, \ 1)$
B. $(1, \ 2, \ -1)$
C. $(-3, \ 4, \ -1)$
D. $(0, \ 1, \ 2)$

30. What is the equation that expresses the relationship between x and y in the table below? *(Average)*

x	y
-2	4
-1	1
0	-2
1	-5
2	-8

A. $y = -x - 2$
B. $y = -3x - 2$
C. $y = 3x - 2$
D. $y = \frac{1}{3}x - 1$

31. **Choose the expression that is not equivalent to 5x + 3y + 15z:**
(Average)

A. 5(x + 3z) + 3y
B. 3(x + y + 5z)
C. 3y + 5(x + 3z)
D. 5x + 3(y + 5z)

32. **Simplify:** $\sqrt{27} + \sqrt{75}$
(Average)

A. $8\sqrt{3}$
B. 34
C. $34\sqrt{3}$
D. $15\sqrt{3}$

33. **What is the equation of the graph below?**
(Rigorous)

A. 2x + y = 2
B. 2x - y = -2
C. 2x - y = 2
D. 2x + y = -2

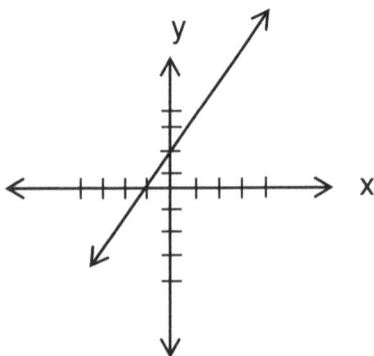

34. $f(x) = 3x - 2;\ f^{-1}(x) =$
(Rigorous)

A. $3x + 2$
B. $x/6$
C. $2x - 3$
D. $(x + 2)/3$

35. **What is the area of a square whose side is 13 feet?**
(Easy)

A. 169 feet
B. 169 square feet
C. 52 feet
D. 52 square feet

36. **The trunk of a tree has a 2.1 meter radius. What is its circumference?**
(Easy)

A. $2.1\,\pi$ square meters
B. $4.2\,\pi$ meters
C. $2.1\,\pi$ meters
D. $4.2\,\pi$ square meters

37. **The figure below shows a running track and the shape of an inscribed rectangle with semicircles at each end.**
(Rigorous)

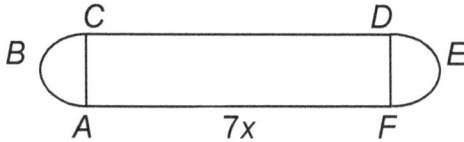

Calculate the distance around the track. (r = 1.5y)

A. $6\pi y + 14x$
B. $3\pi y + 7x$
C. $6\pi y + 7x$
D. $3\pi y + 14x$

38. **What type of triangle is triangle ABC?**
(Easy)

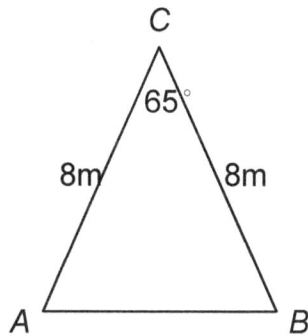

A. right
B. equilateral
C. scalene
D. isosceles

39. **What is the area of this triangle?**
(Easy)

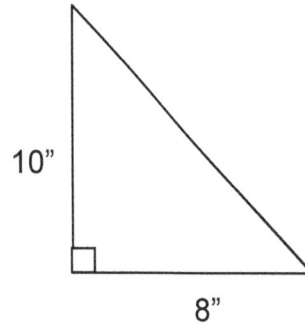

A. 80 square inches
B. 20 square inches
C. 40 square inches
D. 30 square inches

40. **For the following statements**
(Average)

I. **All parallelograms are rectangles**
II. **Some rhombi are squares**

A. Both statements are correct
B. Both statements are incorrect
C. Only II is correct
D. Only I is correct

41. **Find the surface area of a box which is 3 feet wide, 5 feet tall, and 4 feet deep.**
(Average)

A. 47 sq. ft.
B. 60 sq. ft.
C. 94 sq. ft
D. 188 sq. ft.

42. The owner of a rectangular piece of land 40 yards in length and 30 yards in width wants to divide it into two parts. She plans to join two opposite corners with a fence as shown in the diagram below. The cost of the fence will be approximately $25 per linear foot. What is the estimated cost for the fence needed by the owner?
(Rigorous)

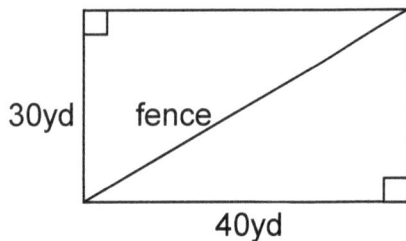

A. $1,250
B. $62,500
C. $5,250
D. $3,750

43. Which term most accurately describes two coplanar lines without any common points?
(Average)

A. perpendicular
B. parallel
C. intersecting
D. skew

44. Set A, B, C, and U are related as shown in the diagram.
(Rigorous)

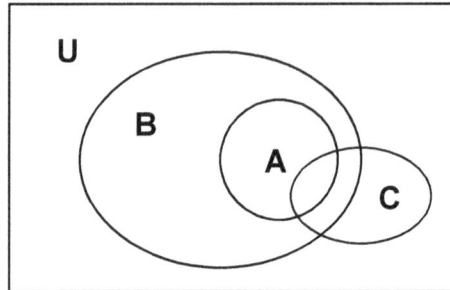

Which of the following is true, assuming not one of the six regions is empty?

A. Any element that is a member of set B is also a member of set A.
B. No element is a member of all three sets A, B, and C.
C. Any element that is a member of set U is also a member of set B.
D. None of the above statements is true.

45. **Select the statement that is the negation of the statement, "If the weather is cold, then the soccer game will be played."**
(Rigorous)

    A. If the weather is not cold, then the soccer game will be played.
    B. The weather is cold and the soccer game was not played.
    C. If the soccer game is played, then the weather is not cold.
    D. The weather is cold and the soccer game will be played.

46. **Select the statement below that is logically equivalent to "If Mary works late, then Bill will prepare lunch."**
(Rigorous)

    A. Bill prepares lunch or Mary does not work late.
    B. If Bill does not prepare lunch, then Mary did not work late.
    C. If Bill prepares lunch, then Mary works late.
    D. Mary does not work late or Bill prepares lunch.

47. **Select the rule of logical equivalence that directly (in one step) transforms the statement (i) into statement (ii),**
(Average)

    i. **Not all the students have books.**
    ii. **Some students do not have books.**

    A. "If p, then q" is equivalent to "if not q, then b."
    B. "Not all are p" is equivalent to "some are not p."
    C. "Not q" is equivalent to "p."
    D. "All are not p" is equivalent to "none are p"

48. **Given that:**

    i. **No athletes are weak.**
    ii. **All football players are athletes.**

    Determine which conclusion can be logically deduced.
(Average)

    A. Some football players are weak.
    B. All football players are weak.
    C. No football player is weak.
    D. None of the above is true.

49. Study the information given below. If a logical conclusion is given, select that conclusion.
(Rigorous)

Bob eats donuts or he eats yogurt. If Bob eats yogurt, then he is healthy. If Bob is healthy, then he can run the marathon. Bob does not eat yogurt.

A. Bob does not eat donuts.
B. Bob is healthy.
C. If Bob runs the marathon then he eats yogurt.
D. None of the above is warranted.

50. Given $K(-4, y)$ and $M(2, -3)$ with midpoint $L(x, 1)$, determine the values of x and y.
(Rigorous)

A. $x = -1, \ y = 5$
B. $x = 3, \ y = 2$
C. $x = 5, \ y = -1$
D. $x = -1, \ y = -1$

Answer Key

1.	D		26.	C
2.	A		27.	A
3.	B		28.	D
4.	D		29.	A
5.	C		30.	B
6.	C		31.	B
7.	B		32.	A
8.	D		33.	B
9.	A		34.	D
10.	B		35.	B
11.	C		36.	B
12.	A		37.	D
13.	B		38.	D
14.	C		39.	C
15.	A		40.	C
16.	D		41.	C
17.	C		42.	D
18.	B		43.	B
19.	C		44.	D
20.	C		45.	B
21.	B		46.	B
22.	C		47.	B
23.	B		48.	C
24.	C		49.	D
25.	A		50.	A

Rigor Table

Easy
2, 14, 16, 18, 20, 22, 35, 36, 38, 39

Average
3, 4, 5, 6, 7, 8, 10, 12, 13, 15, 17, 19, 21, 28, 30, 31, 32, 40, 41, 43, 47, 48

Rigorous
1, 9, 11, 23, 24, 25, 26, 27, 29, 33, 34, 37, 42, 44, 45, 46, 49, 50

MATHEMATICS SAMPLE TEST WITH RATIONALES

1. $\left(\dfrac{^-4}{9}\right) + \left(\dfrac{^-7}{10}\right) =$

   (Rigorous)

   A. $\dfrac{23}{90}$

   B. $\dfrac{^-23}{90}$

   C. $\dfrac{103}{90}$

   D. $\dfrac{^-103}{90}$

Answer: D. $\dfrac{^-103}{90}$

Find the LCD of $\dfrac{^-4}{9}$ and $\dfrac{^-7}{10}$. The LCD is 90, so you get $\dfrac{^-40}{90} + \dfrac{^-63}{90} = \dfrac{^-103}{90}$

2. **0.74 =**
   (Easy)

   A. $\dfrac{74}{100}$

   B. 7.4%

   C. $\dfrac{33}{50}$

   D. $\dfrac{74}{10}$

Answer: A. $\dfrac{74}{100}$

0.74Ⓡ the 4 is in the hundredths place, so the answer is $\dfrac{74}{100}$

3.　　$-9\dfrac{1}{4}$　□　$-8\dfrac{2}{3}$
   (Average)

   A. =
   B. <
   C. >
   D. ≤

Answer: B. <

The larger the absolute value of a negative number, the smaller the negative number is. The absolute value of $-9\dfrac{1}{4}$ is $9\dfrac{1}{4}$ which is larger than the absolute value of $-8\dfrac{2}{3}$, which is $8\dfrac{2}{3}$. Therefore, the relationship should be $-9\dfrac{1}{4} < -8\dfrac{2}{3}$

4.　　**303 is what percent of 600?**
   (Average)

   A. 0.505%
   B. 5.05%
   C. 505%
   D. 50.5%

Answer: D. 50.5%

Use x for the percent. $600x = 303$.　　$\dfrac{600x}{600} = \dfrac{303}{600} \rightarrow x = 0.505 = 50.5\%$

5.　　**An item that sells for \$375 is put on sale at \$120. What is the percent of decrease?**
   (Average)

   A. 25%
   B. 28%
   C. 68%
   D. 34%

Answer: C. 68%

Use $(1 - x)$ as the discount. $375x = 120$.
$375(1 - x) = 120 \rightarrow 375 - 375x = 120 \rightarrow 375x = 255 \rightarrow x = 0.68 = 68\%$

6. **Two mathematics classes have a total of 410 students. The 8:00 am class has 40 more than the 10:00 am class. How many students are in the 10:00 am class?**
(Average)

    A. 123.3
    B. 370
    C. 185
    D. 330

Answer: C. 185
Let x = # of students in the 8 am class and $x - 40$ = # of students in the 10 am class. $x + (x - 40) = 410 \rightarrow 2x - 40 = 410 \rightarrow 2x = 450 \rightarrow x = 225$. So there are 225 students in the 8 am class, and $225 - 40 = 185$ in the 10 am class.

7. **A restaurant employs 465 people. There are 280 waiters and 185 cooks. If 168 waiters and 85 cooks receive pay raises, what percent of the waiters will receive a pay raise?**
(Average)

    A. 36.13%
    B. 60%
    C. 60.22%
    D. 40%

Answer: B. 60%
The total number of waiters is 280 and only 168 of them get a pay raise. Divide the number getting a raise by the total number of waiters to get the percent. $\dfrac{168}{280} = 0.6 = 60\%$

8. $$\frac{7}{9}+\frac{1}{3}\div\frac{2}{3}=$$
    (Average)

    A. $\dfrac{5}{3}$

    B. $\dfrac{3}{2}$

    C. 2

    D. $\dfrac{23}{18}$

Answer: D. $\dfrac{23}{18}$

First, do the division.

$$\frac{1}{3}\div\frac{2}{3}=\frac{1}{3}\times\frac{3}{2}=\frac{1}{2}$$

Add.

$$\frac{7}{9}+\frac{1}{2}=\frac{14}{18}+\frac{9}{18}=\frac{23}{18}$$

9. **Choose the statement that is true for all real numbers.**
    (Rigorous)

    A. $a=0, b\neq 0$, then $\dfrac{b}{a}$ = undefined.

    B. $^-(a+(^-a))=2a$

    C. $2(ab)=^-(2a)b$

    D. $^-a(b+1)=ab-a$

Answer: A. $a=0, b\neq 0$, then $\dfrac{b}{a}$ = undefined.

A is the correct answer because any number divided by 0 is undefined.

10. The price of gas was $3.27 per gallon. Your tank holds 15 gallons of fuel. You are using two tanks a week. How much will you save weekly if the price of gas goes down to $2.30 per gallon? *(Average)*

   A. $26.00
   B. $29.00
   C. $15.00
   D. $17.00

Answer: B. $29.00
15 gallons x 2 tanks = 30 gallons a week
= 30 gallons x $3.27 = $98.10
30 gallons x $2.30 = $69.00
$98.10 - $69.00 = $29.10 is approximately $29.00.

11. In a sample of 40 full-time employees at a particular company, 35 were also holding down a part-time job requiring at least 10 hours/week. If this proportion holds for the entire company of 25000 employees, how many full-time employees at this company are actually holding down a part-time job of at least 10 hours per week? *(Rigorous)*

   A. 714
   B. 625
   C. 21,875
   D. 28,571

Answer: C. 21, 875
$\dfrac{35}{40}$ full time employees have a part time job also. Out of 25,000 full time employees, the number that also have a part time job is
$\dfrac{35}{40} = \dfrac{x}{25000} \rightarrow 40x = 875000 \rightarrow x = 21875$, so 21875 full time employees also have a part time job.

12. **A sofa sells for $520. If the retailer makes a 30% profit, what was the wholesale price?**
(Average)

A. $400
B. $676
C. $490
D. $364

Answer: A. $400
$400; Let x be the wholesale price, then x + .30x = 520, 1.30x = 520. divide both sides by 1.30.

13. **A car gets 25.36 miles per gallon. The car has been driven 83,310 miles. What is a reasonable estimate for the number of gallons of gas used?**
(Average)

A. 2,087 gallons
B. 3,000 gallons
C. 1,800 gallons
D. 164 gallons

Answer: B. 3,000 gallons
Divide the number of miles by the miles per gallon to determine the approximate number of gallons of gas used. $\dfrac{83310 \text{ miles}}{25.36 \text{ miles per gallon}} = 3285$ gallons. This is approximately 3000 gallons.

14. **What unit of measurement could we use to report the distance traveled walking around a track?**
(Easy)

A. degrees
B. square meters
C. kilometers
D. cubic feet

Answer: C. kilometers
Degrees measures angles, square meters measures area, cubic feet measure volume, and kilometers measures length. Kilometers is the only reasonable answer.

15. **What unit of measurement would describe the spread of a forest fire in a unit time?**
(Average)

   A. 10 square yards per second
   B. 10 yards per minute
   C. 10 feet per hour
   D. 10 cubic feet per hour

Answer: A. 10 square yards per second
The only appropriate answer is one that describes "an area" of forest consumed per unit time. All answers are not units of area measurement except answer A.

16. **Express .0000456 in scientific notation.**
(Easy)

   A. $4.56x10^{-4}$
   B. $45.6x10^{-6}$
   C. $4.56x10^{-6}$
   D. $4.56x10^{-5}$

Answer: D. $4.56x10^{-5}$
In scientific notation, the decimal point belongs to the right of the 4, the first significant digit. To get from 4.56 x 10^{-5} back to 0.0000456, we would move the decimal point 5 places to the left.

17. **A student organization is interested in determining how strong the support is among registered voters in the United States for the president's education plan. Which of the following procedures would be most appropriate for selecting a statistically unbiased sample?**
(Average)

   A. Having viewers call in to a nationally broad-cast talk show and give their opinions.
   B. Survey registered voters selected by blind drawing in the three largest states.
   C. Select regions of the country by blind drawing and then select people from the voter's registration list by blind drawing.
   D. Pass out survey forms at the front entrance of schools selected by blind drawing and ask people entering and exiting to fill them in.

Answer: C. Select regions of the country by blind drawing and then select people from the voter's registration list by blind drawing.
C is the best answer because it is random and it surveys a larger population.

18. The following chart shows the yearly average number of international tourists visiting Palm Beach for 1990-1994. How many more international tourists visited Palm Beach in 1994 than in 1991? *(Easy)*

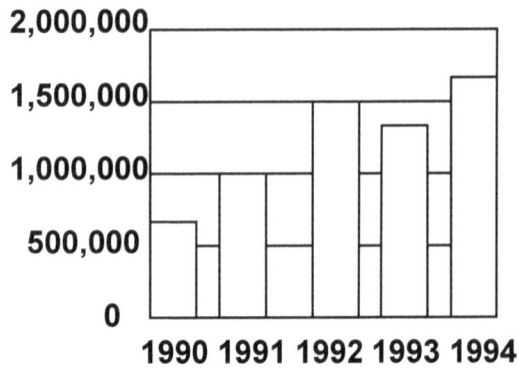

A. 100,000
B. 600,000
C. 1,600,000
D. 8,000,000

Answer: B. 600,000
The number of tourists in 1991 was 1,000,000 and the number in 1994 was 1,600,000. Subtract to get a difference of 600,000.

19. Consider the graph of the distribution of the length of time it took individuals to complete an employment form.
(Average)

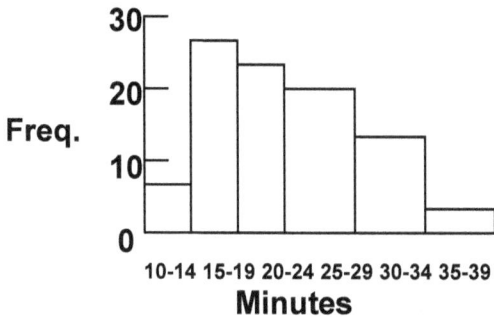

Freq.

Minutes

Approximately how many individuals took less than 15 minutes to complete the employment form?

A. 35
B. 28
C. 7
D. 4

Answer: C. 7
According to the chart, the number of people who took under 15 minutes is 7.

20. Which statement is true about George's budget?
(Easy)

A. George spends the greatest portion of his income on food.
B. George spends twice as much on utilities as he does on his mortgage.
C. George spends twice as much on utilities as he does on food.
D. George spends the same amount on food and utilities as he does on mortgage.

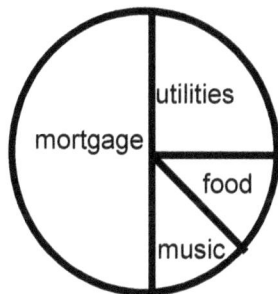

Answer: C. George spends twice as much on utilities as he does on food.
The wedge representing utilities is twice as large as the wedge representing food.

21. **Corporate salaries are listed for several employees. Which is the best measure of central tendency?**
(Average)

$24,000 $24,000 $26,000 $28,000 $30,000 $120,000

   A. Mean
   B. Median
   C. Mode
   D. No difference

Answer: B. Median
The median provides the best measure of central tendency in this case where the mode is the lowest number and the mean is disproportionately skewed by the outlier $120,000.

22. **Compute the median for the following data set:**
(Easy)

{12, 19, 13, 16, 17, 14}

   A. 14.5
   B. 15.17
   C. 15
   D. 16

Answer: C. 15
Arrange the data in ascending order: 12,13,14,16,17,19. The median is the middle value in a list with an odd number of entries. When there is an even number of entries, the median is the mean of the two center entries. Here the average of 14 and 16 is 15.

23. **State the domain of the function** $f(x) = \dfrac{3x-6}{x^2 - 25}$
(Rigorous)

   A. $x \neq 2$
   B. $x \neq 5, -5$
   C. $x \neq 2, -2$
   D. $x \neq 5$

Answer: B. $x \neq 5, -5$
The values of 5 and –5 must be omitted from the domain of all real numbers because if x took on either of those values, the denominator of the fraction would have a value of 0, and therefore the fraction would be undefined.

24. **Which graph represents the equation of** $y = x^2 + 3x$?
   (Rigorous)

A.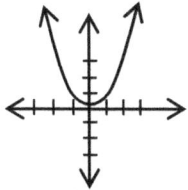

B.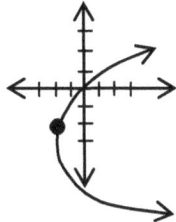

C.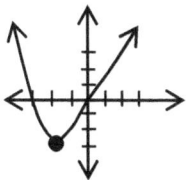

D.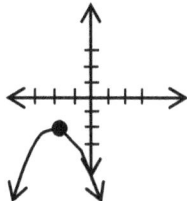

Answer: C.

B is not the graph of a function. D is the graph of a parabola where the coefficient of x^2 is negative. A appears to be the graph of $y = x^2$. To find the x-intercepts of y = x^2 + 3x, set y = 0 and solve for x: 0 = x^2 + 3x = x(x + 3) to get x = 0 or x = -3. Therefore, the graph of the function intersects the x-axis at x=0 and x=-3.

25. Choose the equation that is equivalent to the following: *(Rigorous)*

$$\frac{3x}{5} - 5 = 5x$$

A. $3x - 25 = 25x$

B. $x - \dfrac{25}{3} = 25x$

C. $6x - 50 = 75x$

D. $x + 25 = 25x$

Answer: A. $3x - 25 = 25x$

A is the correct answer because it is the original equation multiplied by 5. The other choices alter the answer to the original equation.

26. If $4x - (3 - x) = 7(x - 3) + 10$, then *(Rigorous)*

A. $x = 8$
B. $x = -8$
C. $x = 4$
D. $x = -4$

Answer: C. *x* = 4

Solve for *x*.

$$4x - (3 - x) = 7(x - 3) + 10$$
$$4x - 3 + x = 7x - 21 + 10$$
$$5x - 3 = 7x - 11$$
$$5x = 7x - 11 + 3$$
$$5x - 7x = {}^{-}8$$
$${}^{-}2x = {}^{-}8$$
$$x = 4$$

27. Solve for x.

$$3x - \frac{2}{3} = \frac{5x}{2} + 2$$

(Rigorous)

A. $5\frac{1}{3}$

B. $\frac{17}{3}$

C. 2

D. $\frac{16}{2}$

Answer: A. $5\frac{1}{3}$

$$3x(6) - \frac{2}{3}(6) = \frac{5x}{2}(6) + 2(6)$$ 6 is the LCD of 2 and 3

$$18x - 4 = 15x + 12$$
$$18x = 15x + 16$$
$$3x = 16$$
$$x = \frac{16}{3} = 5\frac{1}{3}$$

28. **Given the formula *d* =*rt*, (where *d* = distance, *r* =rate, and *t* =time), calculate the time required for a vehicle to travel 585 miles at a rate of 65 miles per hour.**
   (Average)

   A. 8.5 hours
   B. 6.5 hours
   C. 9.5 hours
   D. 9 hours

Answer: D. 9 hours
We are given *d* = 585 miles and *r* = 65 miles per hour and *d* =*rt*. Solve for *t*.
$585 = 65t \rightarrow t = 9$ hours.

29. **Solve the system of equations** for x, y and z.
(Rigorous)

$$3x + 2y - z = 0$$
$$2x + 5y = 8z$$
$$x + 3y + 2z = 7$$

A. $(-1, 2, 1)$
B. $(1, 2, -1)$
C. $(-3, 4, -1)$
D. $(0, 1, 2)$

Answer: A. $(-1, 2, 1)$
Multiplying equation 1 by 2, and equation 2 by –3, and then adding together the two resulting equations gives $-11y + 22z = 0$. Solving for y gives y = 2z. In the meantime, multiplying equation 3 by –2 and adding it to equation 2 gives $-y - 12z = -14$. Then substituting 2z for y, yields the result z = 1. Subsequently, one can easily find that y = 2, and x = -1.

30. **What is the equation that expresses the relationship between x and y in the table below?**
(Average)

x	y
-2	4
-1	1
0	-2
1	-5
2	-8

A. y = -x – 2
B. y = -3x – 2
C. y = 3x – 2
D. $y = \frac{1}{3}x - 1$

Answer: B. y = -3x - 2
Solve by plugging the values of x and y into the equations to see if they work. The answer is B because it is the only equation for which the values of x and y are correct.

31. **Choose the expression that is not equivalent to**
     5x + 3y + 15z:
     (Average)

     A. 5(x + 3z) + 3y
     B. 3(x + y + 5z)
     C. 3y + 5(x + 3z)
     D. 5x + 3(y + 5z)

Answer: B. 3(x + y +5z)

5x + 3y + 15z = (5x + 15z) + 3y = 5(x + 3z) + 3y	A. is true
= 5x + (3y + 15z) = 5x + 3(y + 5z)	D. is true
= 3y + (5x + 15z) = 3y + 5(x + 3z)	C. is true

We can solve all of these using the associative property and then factoring.
However, in B 3(x + y + 5z) by distributive property = 3x + 3y + 15z, which does
not equal 5x + 3y + 15z.

32. **Simplify:** $\sqrt{27} + \sqrt{75}$
     (Average)

     A. $8\sqrt{3}$
     B. 34
     C. $34\sqrt{3}$
     D. $15\sqrt{3}$

Answer: A. $8\sqrt{3}$
Simplifying radicals gives $\sqrt{27} + \sqrt{75} = 3\sqrt{3} + 5\sqrt{3} = 8\sqrt{3}$.

33. **What is the equation of the graph below?**
(Rigorous)

    A. $2x + y = 2$
    B. $2x - y = -2$
    C. $2x - y = 2$
    D. $2x + y = -2$

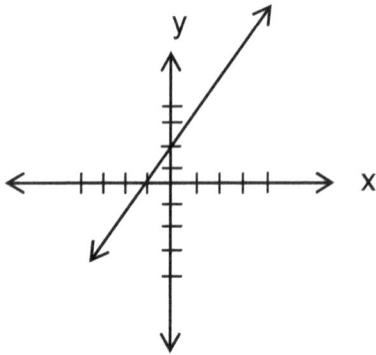

Answer: B. $2x - y = -2$

By observation, we see that the graph has a y-intercept of 2 and a slope of 2/1 = 2. Therefore its equation is y = mx + b = 2x + 2. Rearranging the terms gives 2x – y = -2.

34. $f(x) = 3x - 2; \ f^{-1}(x) =$
(Rigorous)

    A. $3x + 2$
    B. $x / 6$
    C. $2x - 3$
    D. $(x + 2) / 3$

Answer: D. $(x + 2) / 3$

To find the inverse, f⁻¹(x), of the given function, reverse the variables in the given equation, y = 3x – 2, to get x = 3y – 2. Then solve for y as follows:
x+2 = 3y, and y = $\dfrac{x+2}{3}$.

35. **What is the area of a square whose side is 13 feet?**
(Easy)

    A. 169 feet
    B. 169 square feet
    C. 52 feet
    D. 52 square feet

Answer: B. 169 square feet
Area = length times width (*lw*).
Length = 13 feet
Width = 13 feet (square, so length and width are the same).
Area = $13 \times 13 = 169$ square feet.
Area is measured in square feet.

36. **The trunk of a tree has a 2.1 meter radius. What is its circumference?**
(Easy)

    A. 2.1π square meters
    B. 4.2π meters
    C. $2.1\ \pi$ meters
    D. 4.2π square meters

Answer: B. 4.2π meters
Circumference is $2\pi r$, where r is the radius. The circumference is $2\pi 2.1 = 4.2\pi$ meters (not square meters because we are not measuring area).

37. **The figure below shows a running track and the shape of an inscribed rectangle with semicircles at each end.**
   (Rigorous)

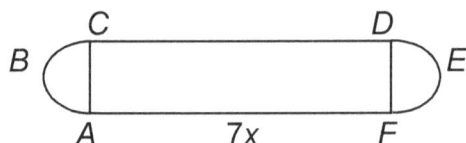

Calculate the distance around the track (r = 1.5y).

   A. $6\pi y + 14x$
   B. $3\pi y + 7x$
   C. $6\pi y + 7x$
   D. $3\pi y + 14x$

Answer: D. $3\pi y + 14x$
The two semicircles of the track create one circle with a diameter 3y. The circumference of a circle is $C = \pi d$ so $C = 3\pi y$. The length of both sides of the track is 7x each side, so the total circumference around the track is $3\pi y + 7x + 7x = 3\pi y + 14x$

38. **What type of triangle is triangle ABC?**
   (Easy)

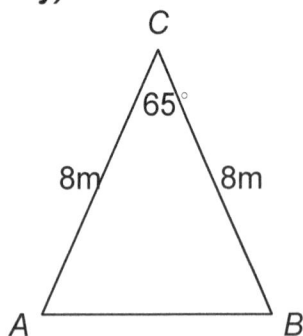

   A. right
   B. equilateral
   C. scalene
   D. isosceles

Answer: D. isosceles
Two of the sides are the same length, so we know the triangle is either equilateral or isosceles. $\angle CAB$ and $\angle CBA$ are equal, because their sides are.

Therefore, $180° = 65° - 2x = \dfrac{115°}{2} = 57.5°$. Because all three angles are not equal, the triangle is isosceles.

39. **What is the area of this triangle?**
(Easy)

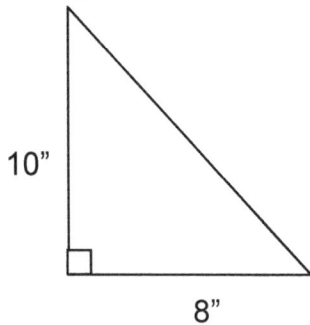

A. 80 square inches
B. 20 square inches
C. 40 square inches
D. 30 square inches

Answer: C. 40 square inches

The area of a triangle is $\frac{1}{2}bh$.

$\frac{1}{2}x8x10 = 40$ square inches.

40. **For the following statements**
(Average)

I. All parallelograms are rectangles
II. Some rhombi are squares

A. Both statements are correct
B. Both statements are incorrect
C. Only II is correct
D. Only I is correct

Answer: C. Only II is correct

I is false because only some parallelograms are rectangles. II is true. So only II is correct.

41. **Find the surface area of a box which is 3 feet wide, 5 feet tall, and 4 feet deep.**
(Average)

    A. 47 sq. ft.
    B. 60 sq. ft.
    C. 94 sq. ft
    D. 188 sq. ft.

Answer: C. 94 sq. ft.
Let's assume the base of the rectangular solid (box) is 3 by 4, and the height is 5. Then the surface area of the top and bottom together is 2(12) = 24. The sum of the areas of the front and back are 2(15) = 30, while the sum of the areas of the sides are 2(20)=40. The total surface area is therefore 94 square feet.

42. **The owner of a rectangular piece of land 40 yards in length and 30 yards in width wants to divide it into two parts. She plans to join two opposite corners with a fence as shown in the diagram below. The cost of the fence will be approximately $25 per linear foot. What is the estimated cost for the fence needed by the owner?**
(Rigorous)

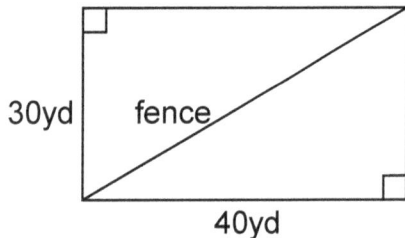

    A. $1,250
    B. $62,500
    C. $5,250
    D. $3,750

Answer: D. $3,750
Find the length of the diagonal by using the Pythagorean theorem. Let x be the length of the diagonal.

$$30^2 + 40^2 = x^2 \rightarrow 900 + 1600 = x^2$$
$$2500 = x^2 \rightarrow \sqrt{2500} = \sqrt{x^2}$$
$$x = 50 \text{ yards}$$

Convert to feet. $\dfrac{50 \text{ yards}}{x \text{ feet}} = \dfrac{1 \text{ yard}}{3 \text{ feet}} \rightarrow 150 \text{ feet}$

It cost $25.00 per linear foot, so the cost is (150 ft) ($25) = $3750.

43. **Which term most accurately describes two coplanar lines without any common points?**
(Average)

    A. perpendicular
    B. parallel
    C. intersecting
    D. skew

Answer: B. parallel
By definition, parallel lines are coplanar lines without any common points.

44. **Set A, B, C, and U are related as shown in the diagram.**
(Rigorous)

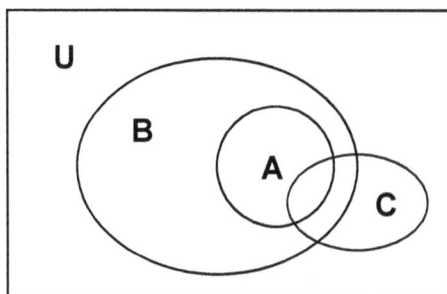

    Which of the following is true, assuming not one of the six regions is empty?

    A. Any element that is a member of set B is also a member of set A.
    B. No element is a member of all three sets A, B, and C.
    C. Any element that is a member of set U is also a member of set B.
    D. None of the above statements is true.

Answer: D. None of the above statements is true.
Answer A is incorrect because not all members of set B are also in set A. Answer B is incorrect because there are elements that are members of all three sets A, B, and C. Answer C is incorrect because not all members of set U are members of set B. This leaves answer D, which states that none of the above choices are true.

45. **Select the statement that is the negation of the statement, "If the weather is cold, then the soccer game will be played."**
(Rigorous)

A. If the weather is not cold, then the soccer game will be played.
B. The weather is cold and the soccer game was not played.
C. If the soccer game is played, then the weather is not cold.
D. The weather is cold and the soccer game will be played.

Answer: B. The weather is cold and the soccer game was not played.
Negation of "if p, then q" is "p and (not q)". So the negation of the given statement is "The weather is cold and the soccer game was not played ".

46. **Select the statement below that is logically equivalent to "If Mary works late, then Bill will prepare lunch."**
(Rigorous)

A. Bill prepares lunch or Mary does not work late.
B. If Bill does not prepare lunch, then Mary did not work late.
C. If Bill prepares lunch, then Mary works late.
D. Mary does not work late or Bill prepares lunch.

Answer: B. If Bill does not prepare lunch, then Mary did not work late.
The contrapositive of a statement is always logically equivalent to the statement. The contrapositive of "if p then q" is "if not q then not p". Since statement B is the contrapositive of the given statement, it is logically equivalent.

The other answer choices assume that if Mary does not work late then Bill does not prepare lunch. This is not a valid deduction from the original statement which merely states that Bill prepares lunch when Mary works late. It does not eliminate the possibility that Bill prepares lunch when Mary does not work late. Hence these statements are not logically equivalent to the given statement.

47. **Select the rule of logical equivalence that directly (in one step) transforms the statement (i) into statement (ii),**
(Average)

i. Not all the students have books.
ii. Some students do not have books.

A. "If p, then q" is equivalent to "if not q, then b."
B. "Not all are p" is equivalent to "some are not p."
C. "Not q" is equivalent to "p."
D. "All are not p" is equivalent to "none are p"

Answer: B. "Not all are p" is equivalent to "some are not p."
If we assume that the statement p is "students have books", then "not p" is "students do not have books". It is clear that statements (i) and (ii) are equivalent to the choice B.

48. **Given that:**

i. No athletes are weak.
ii. All football players are athletes.

Determine which conclusion can be logically deduced.
(Average)

A. Some football players are weak.
B. All football players are weak.
C. No football player is weak.
D. None of the above is true.

Answer: C. No football player is weak.
According to the law of syllogism, "if p then q and if q then r" implies "if p then r". We can rephrase the statements above to read:

i. If a person is a football player, he or she is an athlete.
ii. If a person is an athlete, he or she is not weak.

Then, using the law of syllogism, we can conclude:
If a person is a football player, he or she is not weak.
This statement is equivalent to the one in choice C.

49. **Study the information given below. If a logical conclusion is given, select that conclusion.**
     (Rigorous)

     Bob eats donuts or he eats yogurt. If Bob eats yogurt, then he is healthy. If Bob is healthy, then he can run the marathon. Bob does not eat yogurt.

     A. Bob does not eat donuts.
     B. Bob is healthy.
     C. If Bob runs the marathon then he eats yogurt.
     D. None of the above is warranted.

Answer: D. None of the above is warranted.
Statement A is not warranted since "Bob eats donuts or he eats yogurt" and "Bob does not eat yogurt" implies that "Bob eats donuts".

Statement B is not warranted since according to the given statements, Bob does not eat yogurt and Bob is healthy if he eats yogurt. The statements do not say anything about Bob's health if he does not eat yogurt.

Statement C is not warranted since Bob may run the marathon even if he does not eat yogurt. The given statements do not say anything about Bob's ability to run the marathon if he does not eat yogurt. It merely implies that he can run the marathon if he does eat yogurt.

50. **Given $K(-4, y)$ and $M(2, -3)$ with midpoint $L(x, 1)$, determine the values of x and y.**
     (Rigorous)

     A. $x = -1, y = 5$
     B. $x = 3, y = 2$
     C. $x = 5, y = -1$
     D. $x = -1, y = -1$

Answer: A. $x = -1, y = 5$
The formula for finding the midpoint (a,b) of a segment passing through the points $(x_1, y_1) and (x_2, y_2) is (a, b) = (\dfrac{x_1 + x_2}{2}, \dfrac{y_1 + y_2}{2})$. Setting up the corresponding equations from this information gives us $x = \dfrac{-4 + 2}{2}, and 1 = \dfrac{y - 3}{2}$. Solving for x and y gives x = -1 and y = 5.

ELEMENTS OF COMPOSITION SAMPLE TEST

Directions: The passage below contains many errors. Read the passage. Then, answer each test item by choosing the option that corrects an error in the underlined portion(s). No more than one underlined error will appear in each item. If no error exists, choose "No change is necessary."

Climbing to the top of Mount Everest is an adventure. One which everyone--whether physically fit or not--seems eager to try. The trail stretches for miles, the cold temperatures are usually frigid and brutal.

Climbers must endure severel barriers on the way, including other hikers, steep jagged rocks, and lots of snow. Plus, climbers often find the most grueling part of the trip is their climb back down, just when they are feeling greatly exhausted. Climbers who take precautions are likely to find the ascent less arduous than the unprepared. By donning heavy flannel shirts, gloves, and hats, climbers prevented hypothermia, as well as simple frostbite. A pair of rugged boots is also one of the necesities. If climbers are to avoid becoming dehydrated, there is beverages available for them to transport as well.

Once climbers are completely ready to begin their lengthy journey, they can comfortable enjoy the wonderful scenery. Wide rock formations dazzle the observers eyes with shades of gray and white, while the peak forms a triangle that seems to touch the sky. Each of the climbers are reminded of the splendor and magnificence of God's great Earth.

1. **If climbers are to avoid <u>becoming</u> dehydrated, there <u>is</u> beverages available for <u>them</u> to transport as well.**
   (Rigorous)

   A. becomming
   B. are
   C. him
   D. No change is necessary.

2. **Each of the climbers <u>are</u> reminded of the splendor and <u>magnificence</u> of <u>God's</u> great Earth.**
   (Rigorous)

   A. is
   B. magnifisence
   C. Gods
   D. No change is necessary.

3. **Climbing to the top of Mount Everest is an <u>adventure. One</u> which everyone <u>—whether</u> physically fit or not—<u>seems</u> eager to try.**
   (Average)

   A. adventure, one
   B. everyone, whether
   C. seem
   D. No change is necessary.

4. A pair of rugged boots <u>is also one</u> of the <u>necesities</u>.
(Average)

A. are
B. also, one
C. necessities
D. No change is necessary.

5. Plus, climbers often find the most grueling part of the trip is <u>their</u> climb back <u>down, just</u> when they <u>are</u> feeling greatly exhausted.
(Rigorous)

A. his
B. down; just
C. were
D. No change is necessary.

6. By donning heavy flannel shirts, boots, and <u>hats, climbers prevented</u> hypothermia, as well as simple frostbite.
(Average)

A. hats climbers
B. can prevent
C. hypothermia;
D. No change is necessary.

7. Climbers must endure <u>severel</u> barriers <u>on the way, including</u> other <u>hikers,</u> steep jagged rocks, and lots of snow.
(Average)

A. several
B. on the way: including
C. hikers'
D. No change is necessary.

8. <u>Climbers who</u> take precautions are likely to find the ascent <u>less difficult than</u> the unprepared.
(Easy)

A. Climbers, who
B. least difficult
C. then
D. No change is necessary.

9. Once climbers are completely prepared for <u>their</u> lengthy <u>journey, they</u> can <u>comfortable</u> enjoy the wonderful scenery.
(Easy)

A. they're
B. journey; they
C. comfortably
D. No change is necessary.

10. Wide rock formations dazzle the <u>observers eyes</u> with shades of gray and <u>white, while</u> the peak <u>forms</u> a triangle that seems to touch the sky.
(Average)

A. observers' eyes
B. white; while
C. formed
D. No change is necessary.

11. The <u>trail</u> stretches for <u>miles,</u> the cold temperatures are <u>usually</u> frigid and brutal.
(Rigorous)

A. trails
B. miles;
C. usual
D. No change is necessary.

Directions: The passage below contains several errors. Read the passage. Then, answer each test item by choosing the option that corrects an error in the underlined portion(s). No more than one underlined error will appear in each item. If no error exists, choose "No change is necessary."

Every job places different kinds of demands on their employees. For example, whereas such jobs as accounting and bookkeeping require mathematical ability; graphic design requires creative/artistic ability.

Doing good at one job does not usually guarantee success at another. However, one of the elements crucial to all jobs are especially notable: the chance to accomplish a goal.

The accomplishment of the employees varies according to the job. In many jobs, the employees become accustom to the accomplishment provided by the work they do every day.

In medicine, for example, every doctor tests him self by treating badly injured or critically ill people. In the operating room, a team of Surgeons, is responsible for operating on many of these patients. In addition to the feeling of accomplishment that the workers achieve, some jobs also give a sense of identity to the employees'. Profesions like law, education, and sales offer huge financial and emotional rewards. Politicians are public servants: who work for the federal and state governments.

President obama is basically employed by the American people to make laws and run the country.

Finally; the contributions that employees make to their companies and to the world cannot be taken for granted. Through their work, employees are performing a service for their employers and are contributing something to the world.

12. **Every job places different kinds of demands on their employees.**
     (Average)

     A. place
     B. its
     C. employes
     D. No change is necessary.

13. **However, one of the elements crucial to all jobs are especially notable: the accomplishment of a goal.**
     (Average)

     A. However
     B. is
     C. notable;
     D. No change is necessary.

14. **The accomplishment of the employees varies according to the job.**
     (Average)

     A. accomplishment,
     B. employee's
     C. vary
     D. No change is necessary.

15. <u>Profesions</u> like law, <u>education,</u> and sales <u>offer</u> huge financial and emotional rewards.
(Easy)

A. Professions
B. education;
C. offered
D. No change is necessary.

16. Doing <u>good</u> at one job does not <u>usually</u> guarantee <u>success</u> at another.
(Average)

A. well
B. usualy
C. succeeding
D. No change is necessary.

17. In many jobs, the employees <u>become</u> <u>accustom</u> to the accomplishment <u>provided</u> by the work they do every day.
(Rigorous)

A. became
B. accustomed
C. provides
D. No change is necessary.

18. In medicine, for example, every doctor <u>tests</u> <u>him self</u> by treating badly-injured and critically ill people.
(Easy)

A. test
B. himself
C. critical
D. No change is necessary.

19. In addition to the feeling of accomplishment that the workers <u>achieve</u>, some jobs also <u>give</u> a sense of self-identity to the <u>employees'</u>.
(Average)

A. acheve
B. gave
C. employees
D. No change is necessary.

20. <u>For example, whereas</u> such jobs as accounting and bookkeeping require mathematical <u>ability;</u> graphic design requires creative/artistic ability.
(Rigorous)

A. For example
B. whereas,
C. ability,
D. No change is necessary.

21. In the <u>operating room,</u> a team of <u>Surgeons, is</u> responsible for operating on many of <u>these</u> patients.
(Easy)

A. operating room:
B. surgeons is
C. those
D. No change is necessary.

22. Politicians <u>are</u> public <u>servants: who work</u> for the federal and state governments.
(Average)

A. were
B. servants who
C. worked
D. No change is necessary.

23. President obama is basically employed <u>by</u> the American people to <u>make</u> laws and run the country.
(Easy)

   A. Obama
   B. to
   C. made
   D. No change is necessary.

24. <u>Finally;</u> the contributions that employees make to <u>their</u> companies and to the world cannot be <u>taken</u> for granted.
(Average)

   A. Finally,
   B. thier
   C. took
   D. No change is necessary.

Directions: For the underlined sentence(s), choose the option that expresses the meaning with the most fluency and the clearest logic within the context. If the underlined sentence should not be changed, choose Option A, which shows no change.

25. Which of the following sentences logically and correctly expresses the comparison?
(Rigorous)

   A. The Empire State Building in New York is taller than buildings in the city.
   B. The Empire State Building in New York is taller than any other building in the city.
   C. The Empire State Building in New York is tallest than other buildings in the city.

26. **Treating patients for drug and/or alcohol abuse is a sometimes difficult process. Even though there are a number of different methods for helping the patient overcome a dependency, there is no way of knowing which is best in the long run.**
(Rigorous)

   A. Even though there are a number of different methods for helping the patient overcome a dependency, there is no way of knowing which is best in the long run.
   B. Even though different methods can help a patient overcome a dependency, there is no way to know which is best in the long run.
   C. Even though there is no way to know which way is best in the long run, patients can overcome their dependencies when they are helped.
   D. There is no way to know which method will help the patient overcome a dependency in the long run, even though there are many different ones.

27. **Selecting members of a President's cabinet can often be an aggravating process. Either there are too many or too few qualified candidates for a certain position, and then they have to be confirmed by the Senate, where there is the possibility of rejection.**
(Rigorous)

   A. Either there are too many or too few qualified candidates for a certain position, and then they have to be confirmed by the Senate, where there is the possibility of rejection.
   B. Qualified candidates for certain positions face the possibility of rejection, when they have to be confirmed by the Senate.
   C. The Senate has to confirm qualified candidates, who face the possibility of rejection.
   D. Because the Senate has to confirm qualified candidates; they face the possibility of rejection.

28. **Many factors account for the decline in the quality of public education. <u>Overcrowding, budget cutbacks, and societal deterioration which have greatly affected student learning</u>.**
(Rigorous)

   A. Overcrowding, budget cutbacks, and societal deterioration which have greatly affected student learning.
   B. Student learning has been greatly affected by overcrowding, budget cutbacks, and societal deterioration.
   C. Due to overcrowding, budget cutbacks, and societal deterioration, student learning has been greatly affected.
   D. Overcrowding, budget cutbacks, and societal deterioration have affected students learning greatly.

Directions: Choose the most effective word within the context of the sentence.

29. **Many of the clubs in Boca Raton are noted for their _____ elegance.**
(Average)

   A. vulgar
   B. tasteful
   C. ordinary

30. **When a student is expelled from school, the parents are usually _____ in advance.**
(Easy)

   A. rewarded
   B. congratulated
   C. notified

31. **Before appearing in court, the witness was _____ the papers requiring her to show up.**
(Easy)

   A. condemned
   B. served
   C. criticized

Directions: Choose the underlined word or phrase that is unnecessary within the context of the passage.

32. Considered by many to be one of the worst terrorist incidents on American soil was the bombing of the Oklahoma City Federal Building, which will be remembered for years to come.
(Rigorous)

A. considered by many to be
B. terrorist
C. on American soil
D. for years to come

33. The flu epidemic struck most of the respected faculty and students of The Woolbright School, forcing the Boynton Beach School Superintendent to close it down for two weeks.
(Rigorous)

A. flu
B. most of
C. respected
D. for two weeks

34. The expanding number of television channels has prompted cable operators to raise their prices, even though many consumers do not want to pay a higher increased amount for their service.
(Average)

A. expanding
B. prompted
C. even though
D. increased

Directions: The passage below contains several errors. Read the passage. Then, answer each test item by choosing the option that corrects an error in the underlined portion(s). No more than one underlined error will appear in each item. If no error exists, choose "No change is necessary."

The discovery of a body at Paris Point marina in Boca Raton shocked the residents of Palmetto Pines, a luxury condominium complex located next door to the marina.

The victim is a thirty-five year old woman who had been apparently bludgeoned to death and dumped in the ocean late last night. Many neighbors reported terrible screams, gunshots: as well as the sound of a car backfiring loudly to Boca Raton Police shortly after midnight. The woman had been spotted in the lobby of Palmetto Pines around ten thirty, along with an older man, estimated to be in his fifties, and a younger man, in his late twenties.

"Apparently, the victim had been driven to the complex by the older man and was seen arguing with him when the younger man intervened," said Sheriff Fred Adams, "all three of them left the building together and walked to the marina, where gunshots rang out an hour later." Deputies found five bullets on the sidewalk and some blood, along with a steel pipe that is assumed to be the murder weapon. Two men were seen fleeing the scene in a red Mercedes shortly after, rushing toward the Interstate. The Palm Beach County Coroner, Melvin

Watts, said he concluded the victim's skull had been crushed by a blunt tool, which resulted in a brain hemorrhage. As of now, there is no clear motive for the murder.

35. **The victim <u>is</u> a thirty-five-year-old who had been apparently <u>bludgeoned</u> to death and dumped in the <u>ocean late</u> last night.**
(Rigorous)

   A. was
   B. bludgoned
   C. ocean: late
   D. No change is necessary.

36. **The discovery of a body at Paris Point <u>marina</u> in Boca Raton shocked the <u>residents</u> of Palmetto Pines, a luxury <u>condominium</u> complex located next door to the marina.**
(Rigorous)

   A. Marina
   B. residence
   C. condominnium
   D. No change is necessary.

37. **Deputies found five bullets on the sidewalk and some <u>blood,</u> along with a steel pipe that is <u>assumed</u> <u>to be</u> the murder weapon.**
(Rigorous)

   A. blood;
   B. assuming
   C. to have been
   D. No change is necessary.

38. Many <u>neighbors</u> reported terrible screams, <u>gunshots:</u> <u>as</u> well as the sound of a car, backfiring <u>loudly</u> to Boca Raton Police shortly after midnight.
(Average)

A. nieghbors
B. gunshots, as
C. loud
D. No change is necessary.

39. The woman <u>had</u> been spotted in the lobby of Palmetto Pines around ten <u>thirty,</u> along with an older <u>man, estimated</u> to be in his fifties, and a younger man in his late twenties.
(Average)

A. has
B. thirty;
C. man estimated
D. No change is necessary.

40. "Apparently, the victim had been driven to the complex by the older man and was seen arguing with him when the younger man intervened," said <u>Sheriff Fred Adams, "all</u> three of them left the building together and walked to the marina, where gunshots rang out an hour later."
(Rigorous)

A. sheriff Fred Adams, "all
B. sheriff Fred Adams, "All
C. Sheriff Fred Adams. "All
D. No change is necessary.

Answer Key

1.	B	21.	B
2.	A	22.	B
3.	A	23.	A
4.	C	24.	A
5.	D	25.	B
6.	B	26.	B
7.	A	27.	C
8.	D	28.	B
9.	C	29.	B
10.	A	30.	C
11.	B	31.	B
12.	B	32.	A
13.	B	33.	C
14.	C	34.	D
15.	A	35.	A
16.	A	36.	A
17.	B	37.	C
18.	B	38.	B
19.	C	39.	C
20.	C	40.	C

Rigor Table

Easy
8, 9, 15, 18, 21, 23, 30, 31

Average
3, 4, 6, 7, 10, 12, 13, 14, 16, 19, 22, 24, 29, 34, 38, 39

Rigorous
1, 2, 5, 11, 17, 20, 25, 26, 27, 28, 32, 33, 35, 36, 37, 40

ELEMENTS OF COMPOSITION SAMPLE TEST WITH RATIONALES

Directions: The passage below contains many errors. Read the passage. Then, answer each test item by choosing the option that corrects an error in the underlined portion(s). No more than one underlined error will appear in each item. If no error exists, choose "No change is necessary."

Climbing to the top of Mount Everest is an adventure. One which everyone--whether physically fit or not--seems eager to try. The trail stretches for miles, the cold temperatures are usually frigid and brutal.

Climbers must endure severel barriers on the way, including other hikers, steep jagged rocks, and lots of snow. Plus, climbers often find the most grueling part of the trip is their climb back down, just when they are feeling greatly exhausted. Climbers who take precautions are likely to find the ascent less arduous than the unprepared. By donning heavy flannel shirts, gloves, and hats, climbers prevented hypothermia, as well as simple frostbite. A pair of rugged boots is also one of the necesities. If climbers are to avoid becoming dehydrated, there is beverages available for them to transport as well.

Once climbers are completely ready to begin their lengthy journey, they can comfortable enjoy the wonderful scenery. Wide rock formations dazzle the observers eyes with shades of gray and white, while the peak forms a triangle that seems to touch the sky. Each of the climbers are reminded of the splendor and magnificence of God's great Earth.

1.   **If climbers are to avoid <u>becoming</u> dehydrated, there <u>is</u> beverages available for <u>them</u> to transport as well.**
     (Rigorous)

     A. becommming
     B. are
     C. him
     D. No change is necessary.

Answer: B. are
The plural verb *are* must be used with the plural subject *beverages*. Option A is incorrect because *becoming* has only one *m*. Option C is incorrect because the plural pronoun *them* is needed to agree with the referent *climbers*.

2. **Each of the climbers <u>are</u> reminded of the splendor and <u>magnificence</u> of <u>God's</u> great Earth.**
(Rigorous)

A. is
B. magnifisence
C. Gods
D. No change is necessary.

Answer: A. is
The singular verb *is* agrees with the singular subject *each*. Option B is incorrect because *magnificence* is misspelled. Option C is incorrect because an apostrophe is needed to show possession.

3. **Climbing to the top of Mount Everest is an <u>adventure. One</u> which everyone —<u>whether</u> physically fit or not—<u>seems</u> eager to try.**
(Average)

A. adventure, one
B. everyone, whether
C. seem
D. No change is necessary.

Answer: A. adventure, one
A comma is needed between *adventure* and *one* to avoid creating a fragment of the second part. In Option B, a comma after *everyone* would not be appropriate when the dash is used on the other side of *not*. In Option C, the singular verb *seems* is needed to agree with the singular subject *everyone*.

4. **A pair of rugged boots <u>is also one</u> of the <u>necesities</u>.**
(Average)

A. are
B. also, one
C. necessities
D. No change is necessary.

Answer: C. necessities
The word *necessities* is misspelled in the text. Option A is incorrect because the singular verb *is* must agree with the singular noun *pair* (a collective singular). Option B is incorrect because *is also* is set off with commas (potential correction); it should be set off on both sides.

5. **Plus, climbers often find the most grueling part of the trip is <u>their</u> climb back <u>down, just</u> when they <u>are</u> feeling greatly exhausted.**
(Rigorous)

A. his
B. down; just
C. were
D. No change is necessary.

Answer: D. No change is necessary.
The present tense must be used consistently throughout; therefore, Option C is incorrect. Option A is incorrect because the singular pronoun *his* does not agree with the plural antecedent *climbers*. Option B is incorrect because a comma, not a semicolon, is needed to separate the dependent clause from the main clause.

6. **By donning heavy flannel shirts, boots, and <u>hats, climbers</u> <u>prevented</u> hypothermia, as well as simple frostbite.**
(Average)

A. hats climbers
B. can prevent
C. hypothermia;
D. No change is necessary.

Answer: B. can prevent
The verb *prevented* is in the past tense and must be changed to the present *can prevent* to be consistent. Option A is incorrect because a comma is needed after a long introductory phrase. Option C is incorrect because the semicolon creates a fragment of the phrase *as well as simple frostbite*.

7. **Climbers must endure <u>severel</u> barriers <u>on the way, including</u> other <u>hikers</u>, steep jagged rocks, and lots of snow.**
(Average)

A. several
B. on the way: including
C. hikers'
D. No change is necessary.

Answer: A. several
The word *several* is misspelled in the text. Option B is incorrect because a comma, not a colon, is needed to set off the modifying phrase. Option C is incorrect because no apostrophe is needed after *hikers* since possession is not involved.

8. <u>Climbers who</u> take precautions are likely to find the ascent <u>less difficult</u> <u>than</u> the unprepared.
(Easy)

    A. Climbers, who
    B. least difficult
    C. then
    D. No change is necessary.

Answer: D. No change is necessary.
No change is needed. Option A is incorrect because a comma would make the phrase *who take precautions* seem less restrictive or less essential to the sentence. Option B is incorrect because *less* is appropriate when two items—the prepared and the unprepared—are compared. Option C is incorrect because the comparative adverb *than*, not *then*, is needed.

9. Once climbers are completely prepared for <u>their</u> lengthy <u>journey,</u> <u>they</u> can <u>comfortable</u> enjoy the wonderful scenery.
(Easy)

    A. they're
    B. journey; they
    C. comfortably
    D. No change is necessary.

Answer: C. comfortably
The adverb form *comfortably* is needed to modify the verb phrase *can enjoy*. Option A is incorrect because the possessive plural pronoun is spelled *their*. Option B is incorrect because a semicolon would make the first half of the item seem like an independent clause when the subordinating conjunction *once* makes that clause dependent.

10. Wide rock formations dazzle the <u>observers eyes</u> with shades of gray and <u>white, while</u> the peak <u>forms</u> a triangle that seems to touch the sky.
(Average)

A. observers' eyes
B. white; while
C. formed
D. No change is necessary.

Answer: A. observers' eyes
An apostrophe is needed to show the plural possessive form *observers' eyes*. Option B is incorrect because the semicolon would make the second half of the item seem like an independent clause when the subordinating conjunction *while* makes that clause dependent. Option C is incorrect because *formed* is in the wrong tense.

11. The <u>trail</u> stretches for <u>miles</u>, the cold temperatures are <u>usually</u> frigid and brutal.
(Rigorous)

A. trails
B. miles;
C. usual
D. No change is necessary.

Answer: B. miles;
A semicolon, not a comma, is needed to separate the first independent clause from the second independent clause. Option A is incorrect because the plural subject *trails* needs the singular verb *stretch*. Option C is incorrect because the adverb form *usually* is needed to modify the adjective *frigid.*

Directions: The passage below contains several errors. Read the passage. Then, answer each test item by choosing the option that corrects an error in the underlined portion(s). No more than one underlined error will appear in each item. If no error exists, choose "No change is necessary."

Every job places different kinds of demands on their employees. For example, whereas such jobs as accounting and bookkeeping require mathematical ability; graphic design requires creative/artistic ability.

Doing good at one job does not usually guarantee success at another. However, one of the elements crucial to all jobs are especially notable: the chance to accomplish a goal.

The accomplishment of the employees varies according to the job. In many jobs, the employees become accustom to the accomplishment provided by the work they do every day.

In medicine, for example, every doctor tests him self by treating badly injured or critically ill people. In the operating room, a team of Surgeons, is responsible for operating on many of these patients. In addition to the feeling of accomplishment that the workers achieve, some jobs also give a sense of identity to the employees'. Profesions like law, education, and sales offer huge financial and emotional rewards. Politicians are public servants: who work for the federal and state governments. President obama is basically employed by the American people to make laws and run the country.

Finally; the contributions that employees make to their companies and to the world cannot be taken for granted. Through their work, employees are performing a service for their employers and are contributing something to the world.

12. **Every job places different kinds of demands on their employees.** *(Average)*

   A. place
   B. its
   C. employes
   D. No change is necessary.

Answer: B. its
The singular possessive pronoun *its* must agree with its antecedent *job*, which is singular also. Option A is incorrect because *place* is a plural form, and the subject, *job*, is singular. Option C is incorrect because the correct spelling of employees is given in the sentence.

13. **However,** one of the elements crucial to all jobs **are** especially **notable:** the accomplishment of a goal.
(Average)

   A. However
   B. is
   C. notable;
   D. No change is necessary.

Answer: B. is
The singular verb *is* is needed to agree with the singular subject *one*. Option A is incorrect because a comma is needed to set off the transitional word *however*. Option C is incorrect because a colon, not a semicolon, is needed to set off an item.

14. The **accomplishment** of the **employees** **varies** according to the job.
(Average)

   A. accomplishment,
   B. employee's
   C. vary
   D. No change is necessary.

Answer: C. vary
The singular verb *vary* is needed to agree with the singular subject *accomplishment*. Option A is incorrect because a comma after *accomplishment* would suggest that the modifying phrase *of the employees* is additional instead of essential. Option B is incorrect because *employees* is not possessive.

15. **Profesions** like law, **education,** and sales **offer** huge financial and emotional rewards.
(Easy)

   A. Professions
   B. education;
   C. offered
   D. No change is necessary.

Answer: A. Professions
Option A is correct because *professions* is misspelled in the sentence. Option B is incorrect because a comma, not a semi-colon, is needed after *education*. In Option C, *offered* is in the wrong tense.

16.   Doing <u>good</u> at one job does not <u>usually</u> guarantee <u>success</u> at another.
(Average)

   A. well
   B. usualy
   C. succeeding
   D. No change is necessary.

Answer: A. well
The adverb *well* modifies the word *doing*. Option B is incorrect because *usually* is spelled correctly in the sentence. Option C is incorrect because *succeeding* is in the wrong tense.

17.   In many jobs, the employees <u>become</u> <u>accustom</u> to the accomplishment <u>provided</u> by the work they do every day.
(Rigorous)

   A. became
   B. accustomed
   C. provides
   D. No change is necessary.

Answer: B. accustomed
The past participle *accustomed* is needed with the verb *become*. Option A is incorrect because the verb tense does not need to change to the past *became*. Option C is incorrect because *provides* is the wrong tense.

18.   In medicine, for example, every doctor <u>tests</u> <u>him self</u> by treating badly-injured and critically ill people.
(Easy)

   A. test
   B. himself
   C. critical
   D. No change is necessary.

Answer: B. himself
The reflexive pronoun *himself* is needed. (Him self is nonstandard and never correct.) Option A is incorrect because the singular verb *test* is needed to agree with the singular subject *doctor*. Option C is incorrect because the adverb *critically* is needed to modify the verb *ill*.

19. **In addition to the feeling of accomplishment that the workers achieve, some jobs also give a sense of self-identity to the employees'.**
(Average)

   A. acheve
   B. gave
   C. employees
   D. No change is necessary.

Answer: C. employees
Option C is correct because *employees* is not possessive. Option A is incorrect because *achieve* is spelled correctly in the sentence. Option B is incorrect because *gave* is the wrong tense.

20. **For example, whereas such jobs as accounting and bookkeeping require mathematical ability; graphic design requires creative/artistic ability.**
(Rigorous)

   A. For example
   B. whereas,
   C. ability,
   D. No change is necessary.

Answer: C. ability,
An introductory dependent clause is set off with a comma, not a semicolon. Option A is incorrect because the transitional phrase *for example* should be set off with a comma. Option B is incorrect because the adverb *whereas* functions like *while* and does not take a comma after it.

21. **In the operating room, a team of Surgeons, is responsible for operating on many of these patients.**
(Easy)

   A. operating room:
   B. surgeons is
   C. those
   D. No change is necessary.

Answer: B. surgeons is
Surgeons is not a proper name, so it does not need to be capitalized. A comma is not needed to break up *a team of surgeons* from the rest of the sentence. Option A is incorrect because a comma, not a colon, is needed to set off an item. Option C is incorrect because *those* is an incorrect pronoun.

22. Politicians <u>are</u> public <u>servants: who</u> <u>work</u> for the federal and state governments.
(Average)

   A. were
   B. servants who
   C. worked
   D. No change is necessary.

Answer: B. servants who
A colon is not needed to set off the introduction of the sentence. In Option A, *were* is the incorrect tense of the verb. In Option C, *worked* is in the wrong tense.

23. President obama is basically employed <u>by</u> the American people to <u>make</u> laws and run the country.
(Easy)

   A. Obama
   B. to
   C. made
   D. No change is necessary.

Answer: A. Obama
Obama is a proper name and should be capitalized. In Option B, *to* does not fit with the verb *employed*. Option C uses the wrong form of the verb *make*.

24. <u>Finally;</u> the contributions that employees make to <u>their</u> companies and to the world cannot be <u>taken</u> for granted.
(Average)

   A. Finally,
   B. thier
   C. took
   D. No change is necessary.

Answer: A. Finally,
A comma is needed to separate *Finally* from the rest of the sentence. *Finally* is a preposition which usually heads a dependent sentence, hence a comma is needed. Option B is incorrect because *their* is misspelled. Option C is incorrect because *took* is the wrong form of the verb.

Directions: For the underlined sentence(s), choose the option that expresses the meaning with the most fluency and the clearest logic within the context. If the underlined sentence should not be changed, choose Option A, which shows no change.

25. **Which of the following sentences logically and correctly expresses the comparison?**
(Rigorous)

A. The Empire State Building in New York is taller than buildings in the city.
B. The Empire State Building in New York is taller than any other building in the city.
C. The Empire State Building in New York is tallest than other buildings in the city.

Answer: B. The Empire State Building in New York is taller than any other building in the city.
Because the Empire State Building is a building in New York City, the phrase *any other* must be included. Option A is incorrect because the Empire State Building is implicitly compared to itself since it is one of the buildings. Option C is incorrect because *tallest* is the incorrect form of the adjective.

26. **Treating patients for drug and/or alcohol abuse is a sometimes difficult process. <u>Even though there are a number of different methods for helping the patient overcome a dependency, there is no way of knowing which is best in the long run.</u>**
(Rigorous)

A. Even though there are a number of different methods for helping the patient overcome a dependency, there is no way of knowing which is best in the long run.
B. Even though different methods can help a patient overcome a dependency, there is no way to know which is best in the long run.
C. Even though there is no way to know which way is best in the long run, patients can overcome their dependencies when they are helped.
D. There is no way to know which method will help the patient overcome a dependency in the long run, even though there are many different ones.

Answer: B. Even though different methods can help a patient overcome a dependency, there is no way to know which is best in the long run.
Option B is concise and logical. Option A tends to ramble with the use of *there are* and the verbs *helping* and *knowing*. Option C is awkwardly worded and repetitive in the first part of the sentence, and vague in the second because it never indicates how the patients can be helped. Option D contains the unnecessary phrase *even though there are many different ones.*

27. Selecting members of a President's cabinet can often be an aggravating process. <u>Either there are too many or too few qualified candidates for a certain position, and then they have to be confirmed by the Senate, where there is the possibility of rejection.</u>
(Rigorous)

    A. Either there are too many or too few qualified candidates for a certain position, and then they have to be confirmed by the Senate, where there is the possibility of rejection.
    B. Qualified candidates for certain positions face the possibility of rejection, when they have to be confirmed by the Senate.
    C. The Senate has to confirm qualified candidates, who face the possibility of rejection.
    D. Because the Senate has to confirm qualified candidates; they face the possibility of rejection.

Answer: C. The Senate has to confirm qualified candidates, who face the possibility of rejection.
Option C is the most straightforward and concise sentence. Option A is too unwieldy with the wordy *Either...or* phrase at the beginning. Option B doesn't make clear the fact that candidates face rejection by the Senate. Option D illogically implies that candidates face rejection because they have to be confirmed by the Senate.

28. Many factors account for the decline in the quality of public education. <u>Overcrowding, budget cutbacks, and societal deterioration which have greatly affected student learning</u>.
(Rigorous)

    A. Overcrowding, budget cutbacks, and societal deterioration which have greatly affected student learning.
    B. Student learning has been greatly affected by overcrowding, budget cutbacks, and societal deterioration.
    C. Due to overcrowding, budget cutbacks, and societal deterioration, student learning has been greatly affected.
    D. Overcrowding, budget cutbacks, and societal deterioration have affected students learning greatly.

Answer: B. Student learning has been greatly affected by overcrowding, budget cutbacks, and societal deterioration.
Option B is concise and best explains the causes of the decline in student education. The unnecessary use of *which* in Option A makes the sentence feel incomplete. Option C has weak coordination between the reasons for the decline in public education and the fact that student learning has been affected. Option D incorrectly places the adverb *greatly* after learning, instead of before *affected.*

Directions: Choose the most effective word within the context of the sentence.

29. **Many of the clubs in Boca Raton are noted for their _____ elegance.**
    (Average)

    A. vulgar
    B. tasteful
    C. ordinary

Answer: B. tasteful
Tasteful means beautiful or charming, which would correspond to an elegant club. The words *vulgar* and *ordinary* have negative connotations.

30. **When a student is expelled from school, the parents are usually _____ in advance.**
    (Easy)

    A. rewarded
    B. congratulated
    C. notified

Answer: C. notified
Notified means informed or told, which fits into the logic of the sentence. The words *rewarded* and *congratulated* are positive actions, which don't make sense regarding someone being expelled from school.

31. **Before appearing in court, the witness was _____ the papers requiring her to show up.**
    (Easy)

    A. condemned
    B. served
    C. criticized

Answer: B. served
Served means given, which makes sense in the context of the sentence. *Condemned* and *criticized* do not make sense within the context of the sentence.

Directions: Choose the underlined word or phrase that is unnecessary within the context of the passage.

32. <u>Considered by many to be</u> one of the worst <u>terrorist</u> incidents <u>on American soil</u> was the bombing of the Oklahoma City Federal Building, which will be remembered <u>for years to come</u>. *(Rigorous)*

    A. considered by many to be
    B. terrorist
    C. on American soil
    D. for years to come

Answer: A. considered by many to be
Considered by many to be is a wordy phrase and unnecessary in the context of the sentence. All other words are necessary within the context of the sentence.

33. The <u>flu</u> epidemic struck <u>most of</u> the <u>respected</u> faculty and students of The Woolbright School, forcing the Boynton Beach School Superintendent to close it down <u>for two weeks.</u> *(Rigorous)*

    A. flu
    B. most of
    C. respected
    D. for two weeks

Answer: C. respected
The fact that the faculty might have been *respected* is not really necessary to mention in the sentence. The other words and phrases are all necessary to complete the meaning of the sentence. The correct answer is C.

34. The <u>expanding</u> number of television channels has <u>prompted</u> cable operators to raise their prices, <u>even though</u> many consumers do not want to pay a higher <u>increased</u> amount for their service. *(Average)*

    A. expanding
    B. prompted
    C. even though
    D. increased

Answer: D. increased
The word *increased* is redundant with *higher* and should be removed. All the other words are necessary within the context of the sentence.

Directions: The passage below contains several errors. Read the passage. Then, answer each test item by choosing the option that corrects an error in the underlined portion(s). No more than one underlined error will appear in each item. If no error exists, choose "No change is necessary."

The discovery of a body at Paris Point marina in Boca Raton shocked the residents of Palmetto Pines, a luxury condominium complex located next door to the marina.

The victim is a thirty-five year old woman who had been apparently bludgeoned to death and dumped in the ocean late last night. Many neighbors reported terrible screams, gunshots: as well as the sound of a car backfiring loudly to Boca Raton Police shortly after midnight. The woman had been spotted in the lobby of Palmetto Pines around ten thirty, along with an older man, estimated to be in his fifties, and a younger man, in his late twenties.

"Apparently, the victim had been driven to the complex by the older man and was seen arguing with him when the younger man intervened," said Sheriff Fred Adams, "all three of them left the building together and walked to the marina, where gunshots rang out an hour later." Deputies found five bullets on the sidewalk and some blood, along with a steel pipe that is assumed to be the murder weapon. Two men were seen fleeing the scene in a red Mercedes shortly after, rushing toward the Interstate. The Palm Beach County Coroner, Melvin Watts, said he concluded the victim's skull had been crushed by a blunt tool, which resulted in a brain hemorrhage. As of now, there is no clear motive for the murder.

35.   The victim <u>is</u> a thirty-five-year-old who had been apparently <u>bludgeoned</u> to death and dumped in the <u>ocean late</u> last night. *(Rigorous)*

        A. was
        B. bludgoned
        C. ocean: late
        D. No change is necessary.

Answer: A. was
The past tense *was* is needed to maintain consistency. Option B creates a misspelling. Option C incorrectly uses a colon when none is needed.

36. The discovery of a body at Paris Point <u>marina</u> in Boca Raton shocked the <u>residents</u> of Palmetto Pines, a luxury <u>condominium</u> complex located next door to the marina.
(Rigorous)

    A. Marina
    B. residence
    C. condominnium
    D. No change is necessary.

Answer: A. Marina
Marina is a name that needs to be capitalized. Options B and C create misspellings.

37. Deputies found five bullets on the sidewalk and some <u>blood,</u> along with a steel pipe that is <u>assumed</u> <u>to be</u> the murder weapon.
(Rigorous)

    A. blood;
    B. assuming
    C. to have been
    D. No change is necessary.

Answer: C. to have been
The past tense *to have been* is needed to maintain consistency. Option A incorrectly uses a semicolon, instead of a comma. Option B uses the wrong form of the verb *assumed*.

38. Many <u>neighbors</u> reported terrible screams, <u>gunshots: as</u> well as the sound of a car, backfiring <u>loudly</u> to Boca Raton Police shortly after midnight.
(Average)

    A. nieghbors
    B. gunshots, as
    C. loud
    D. No change is necessary.

Answer: B. gunshots, as
Option B correctly uses a comma, not a colon to separate the items. Option A creates a misspelling. Option C incorrectly changes the adverb into an adjective.

39. **The woman <u>had</u> been spotted in the lobby of Palmetto Pines around ten <u>thirty,</u> along with an older <u>man, estimated</u> to be in his fifties, and a younger man in his late twenties.**
(Average)

A. has
B. thirty;
C. man estimated
D. No change is necessary.

Answer: C. man estimated
A comma is not needed to separate the item because *an older man estimated to be in his fifties* is one complete fragment. Option A incorrectly uses the present tense *has* instead of the past tense *had*. Option B incorrectly uses a colon when a comma is needed.

40. **"Apparently, the victim had been driven to the complex by the older man and was seen arguing with him when the younger man intervened," said <u>Sheriff Fred Adams, "all</u> three of them left the building together and walked to the marina, where gunshots rang out an hour later."**
(Rigorous)

A. sheriff Fred Adams, "all
B. sheriff Fred Adams, "All
C. Sheriff Fred Adams. "All
D. No change is necessary.

Answer: C. Sheriff Fred Adams. "All
The quote's source comes in the middle of two independent clauses, so a period should follow *Adams*. Option A is incorrect because titles, when they come before a name, must be capitalized. Punctuation is also faulty. Option B is incorrect because the word *Adams* ends a sentence; a comma is not strong enough to support two sentences.

TExES PEDAGOGY AND PROFESSIONAL RESPONSIBILITIES EC-12

SAMPLE TEST

Directions: Read each item and select the best response.

1. **What developmental patterns should a professional teacher assess to meet the needs of the student?**
   (Average)

   A. Academic, regional, and family background
   B. Social, physical, and cognitive
   C. Academic, physical, and family background
   D. Physical, family, and ethnic background

2. **According to Piaget, what stage is characterized by the ability to think abstractly and to use logic?**
   (Easy)

   A. Concrete operations
   B. Pre-operational
   C. Formal operations
   D. Conservative operational

3. **At approximately what age is the average child able to define abstract terms such as honesty and justice?**
   (Rigorous)

   A. 10–12 years old
   B. 4–6 years old
   C. 14–16 years old
   D. 6–8 years old

4. **What would improve planning for instruction?**
   (Average)

   A. Describe the role of the teacher and student
   B. Evaluate the outcomes of instruction
   C. Rearrange the order of activities
   D. Give outside assignments

5. **What is the most significant development emerging in children at age two?**
   (Easy)

   A. Immune system develops
   B. Socialization occurs
   C. Language develops
   D. Perception develops

6. **You are leading a substance abuse discussion for health class. The students present their belief that marijuana is not harmful to their health. What set of data would refute their claim?**
(Rigorous)

   A. It is more carcinogenic than nicotine, lowers resistance to infection, worsens acne, and damages brain cells
   B. It damages brain cells, causes behavior changes in prenatally exposed infants, leads to other drug abuse, and causes short-term memory loss
   C. It lowers tolerance for frustration, causes eye damage, increases paranoia, and lowers resistance to infection
   D. It leads to abusing alcohol, lowers white blood cell count, reduces fertility, and causes gout

7. **Bobby, a nine-year-old, has been caught stealing frequently in the classroom. What might be a factor contributing to this behavior?**
(Average)

   A. Need for the items stolen
   B. Serious emotional disturbance
   C. Desire to experiment
   D. A normal stage of development

8. **What strategy can teachers incorporate in their classrooms that will allow students to acquire the same academic skills even though the students are at various learning levels?**
(Rigorous)

   A. Create learning modules
   B. Apply concrete rules to abstract theories
   C. Incorporate social learning skills
   D. Follow cognitive development progression

9. **The process approach is a three-phase model approach that aims directly at the enhancement of self concept among students. Which of the following are components of this process approach?**
(Rigorous)

   A. Sensing function, transforming function, acting function
   B. Diversity model, ethnicity model, economic model
   C. Problem approach, acting function, diversity model
   D. Ethnicity approach, sensing model, problem approach

10. **Andy shows up to class abusive and irritable. He is often late, sleeps in class, sometimes slurs his speech, and has an odor of drinking. What is the first intervention to take?**
(Rigorous)

A. Confront him, relying on a trusting relationship you think you have
B. Do a lesson on alcohol abuse, making an example of him
C. Do nothing, it is better to err on the side of failing to identify substance abuse
D. Call administration, avoid conflict, and supervise others carefully

11. **What is a good strategy for teaching ethnically diverse students?**
(Average)

A. Do not focus on the students' culture
B. Expect them to assimilate easily into your classroom
C. Imitate their speech patterns
D. Include ethnic studies in the curriculum

12. **Which of the following is an accurate description of an English Language Learner student?**
(Average)

A. Remedial students
B. Exceptional education students
C. Are not a homogeneous group
D. Feel confident in communicating in English when with their peers

13. **What is an effective way to help an English Language Learner student succeed in class?**
(Average)

A. Refer the child to a specialist
B. Maintain an encouraging, success-oriented atmosphere
C. Help them assimilate by making them use English exclusively
D. Help them cope with the content materials you presently use

14. **Johnny, a middle-schooler, comes to class uncharacteristically tired, distracted, withdrawn, and sullen and cries easily. What should be the teacher's first response?**
(Average)

A. Send him to the office to sit
B. Call his parents
C. Ask him what is wrong
D. Ignore his behavior

15. **What should be considered when evaluating textbooks for content?**
(Easy)

    A. Type of print used
    B. Number of photographs used
    C. Free of cultural stereotyping
    D. Outlines at the beginning of each chapter

16. **What steps are important in the review of subject matter in the classroom?**
(Rigorous)

    A. A lesson-initiating review, topic, and a lesson-end review
    B. A preview of the subject matter, an in-depth discussion, and a lesson-end review
    C. A rehearsal of the subject matter and a topic summary within the lesson
    D. A short paragraph synopsis of the previous day's lesson and a written review at the end of the lesson

17. **What are critical elements of the instructional process?**
(Rigorous)

    A. Content, goals, teacher needs
    B. Means of getting money to regulate instruction
    C. Content, materials, activities, goals, learner needs
    D. Materials, definitions, assignments

18. **The teacher states that the lesson the students will be engaged in will consist of a review of the material from the previous day, a demonstration of the scientific principles of an electronic circuit, and small group work on setting up an electronic circuit. What has the teacher demonstrated?**
(Rigorous)

    A. The importance of reviewing
    B. Giving the general framework for the lesson to facilitate learning
    C. Giving students the opportunity to leave if they are not interested in the lesson
    D. Providing momentum for the lesson

19. **What is one component of the instructional planning model that must be given careful evaluation?**
(Rigorous)

    A. Students' prior knowledge and skills
    B. The script the teacher will use in instruction
    C. Future lesson plans
    D. Parent participation

20. **How many stages of intellectual development does Piaget define?**
(Average)

    A. Two
    B. Four
    C. Six
    D. Eight

21. **Who developed the theory of multiple intelligences?**
(Average)

A. Bruner
B. Gardner
C. Kagan
D. Cooper

22. **What is an example of a low order question?**
(Easy)

A. "Why is it important to recycle items in your home?"
B. "Compare how glass and plastics are recycled"
C. "What items do we recycle in our county?"
D. "Explain the importance of recycling in our county"

23. **Bloom's taxonomy references six skill levels within the cognitive domain. The top three skills are known as higher-order thinking skills (HOTS). Which of the following are the three highest order skills?**
(Rigorous)

A. Comprehension, application, analysis
B. Knowledge, comprehension, evaluation
C. Application, synthesis, comprehension
D. Analysis, synthesis, and evaluation

24. **Teachers have a responsibility to help students learn how to organize their classroom environments. Which of the following is NOT an effective method of teaching responsibility to students?**
(Rigorous)

A. Dividing responsibilities among students
B. Doing "spot-checks" of notebooks
C. Cleaning up after students leave the classroom
D. Expecting students to keep weekly calendars

25. **How can students use a computer desktop publishing center?**
(Easy)

A. To set up a classroom budget
B. To create student made books, reports, essays, and more
C. To design a research project
D. To create a classroom behavior management system

26. **Which of the following is considered a study skill?**
(Average)

A. Using graphs, tables, and maps
B. Using a desktop publishing program
C. Explaining important vocabulary words
D. Asking for clarification

27. According to research, what can be a result of specific teacher actions on behavior?
(Rigorous)

A. Increase in student misconduct
B. Increase in the number of referrals
C. Decrease in student participation
D. Decrease in student retentions

28. When using a kinesthetic approach, what would be an appropriate activity?
(Average)

A. List
B. Match
C. Define
D. Debate

29. How can the teacher establish a positive climate in the classroom?
(Average)

A. Help students see the unique contributions of individual differences
B. Use whole group instruction for all content areas
C. Help students divide into cooperative groups based on ability
D. Eliminate teaching strategies that allow students to make choices

30. How can the teacher help students become more work-oriented and less disruptive?
(Rigorous)

A. Seek their input for content instruction
B. Challenge the students with a task and show genuine enthusiasm for it
C. Use behavior modification techniques with all students
D. Make sure lesson plans are complete for the week

31. What has been established to increase student originality, intrinsic motivation, and higher-order thinking skills?
(Rigorous)

A. Classroom climate
B. High expectations
C. Student choice
D. Use of authentic learning opportunities

32. Which of the following is NOT a component of the invitational learning theory?
(Rigorous)

A. Proper arrangement of classroom furniture
B. Adequate ventilation and classroom lighting
C. The regular use of substitute teachers
D. Neutral hues for coloration of walls

33. **How can student misconduct be redirected at times?**
(Easy)

A. The teacher threatens the students
B. The teacher assigns detention to the whole class
C. The teacher stops the activity and stares at the students
D. The teacher effectively handles changing from one activity to another

34. **The concept of efficient use of time includes which of the following?**
(Rigorous)

A. Daily review, seatwork, and recitation of concepts
B. Lesson initiation, transition, and comprehension check
C. Review, test, and review
D. Punctuality, management transition, and wait time avoidance

35. **Reducing off-task time and maximizing the amount of time students spend attending to academic tasks is closely related to which of the following?**
(Rigorous)

A. Using whole class instruction only
B. Business-like behaviors of the teacher
C. Dealing only with major teaching functions
D. Giving students a maximum of two minutes to come to order

36. **What do cooperative learning methods all have in common?**
(Rigorous)

A. Philosophy
B. Cooperative task/cooperative reward structures
C. Student roles and communication
D. Teacher roles

37. **The use of volunteers and paraprofessionals within a classroom enriches the setting by:**
(Easy)

A. Providing more opportunity for individual student attention
B. Offering a perceived sense of increased security for students
C. Modifying the behavior of students
D. All of the above

38. **What is the definition of proactive classroom management?**
(Rigorous)

A. Management that is constantly changing
B. Management that is downplayed
C. Management that gives clear and explicit instructions and rewards compliance
D. Management that is designed by the students

39. **Which of the following significantly increases appropriate behavior in the classroom?**
(Average)

   A. Monitoring the halls
   B. Having class rules
   C. Having class rules, giving feedback, and having individual consequences
   D. Having class rules, and giving feedback

40. **What have recent studies regarding effective teachers concluded?**
(Average)

   A. Effective teachers let students establish rules
   B. Effective teachers establish routines by the sixth week of school
   C. Effective teachers state their own policies and establish consistent class rules and procedures on the first day of class
   D. Effective teachers establish flexible routines

41. **What is one way of effectively managing student conduct?**
(Average)

   A. State expectations about behavior
   B. Let students discipline their peers
   C. Let minor infractions of the rules go unnoticed
   D. Increase disapproving remarks

42. **When is utilization of instructional materials most effective?**
(Average)

   A. When the activities are organized and sequenced
   B. When the materials are prepared weeks in advance
   C. When the students choose the pages to work on
   D. When the students create the instructional materials

43. **Why is it important for a teacher to pose a question before calling on students to answer?**
(Rigorous)

   A. It helps manage student conduct
   B. It keeps the students as a group focused on the class work
   C. It allows students time to collaborate
   D. It gives the teacher time to walk among the students

44. **Wait-time has what effect?**
(Average)

   A. Gives structure to the class discourse
   B. Fewer chain and low-level questions are asked with more high-level questions included
   C. Gives the students time to evaluate the response
   D. Gives the opportunity for in-depth discussion about the topic

45. **What is one benefit of amplifying a student's response?**
(Rigorous)

A. It helps the student develop a positive self-image
B. It is helpful to other students who are in the process of learning the reasoning or steps in answering the question
C. It allows the teacher to cover more content
D. It helps to keep the information organized

46. **What is not a way that teachers show acceptance and give value to a student response?**
(Rigorous)

A. Acknowledging
B. Correcting
C. Discussing
D. Amplifying

47. **What is an effective amount of wait-time?**
(Easy)

A. 1 second
B. 5 seconds
C. 15 seconds
D. 10 seconds

48. **Ms. Smith says, "Yes, exactly what do you mean by 'It was the author's intention to mislead you'" What does this illustrate?**
(Rigorous)

A. Digression
B. Restates response
C. Probes a response
D. Amplifies a response

49. **The teacher responds, "Yes, that is correct" to a student's answer. What is this an example of?**
(Average)

A. Academic feedback
B. Academic praise
C. Simple positive response
D. Simple negative response

50. **When are students more likely to understand complex ideas?**
(Rigorous)

A. If they do outside research before coming to class
B. Later when they write out the definitions of complex words
C. When they attend a lecture on the subject
D. When they are clearly defined by the teacher and are given examples and non-examples of the concept

51. **What are the two ways concepts can be taught?**
(Easy)

A. Factually and interpretively
B. Inductively and deductively
C. Conceptually and inductively
D. Analytically and facilitatively

52. **According to Piaget, when does the development of symbolic functioning and language take place?**
(Average)

A. Concrete operations stage
B. Formal operations stage
C. Sensorimotor stage
D. Preoperational stage

53. **What should a teacher do when students have not responded well to an instructional activity?**
(Average)

A. Reevaluate learner needs
B. Request administrative help
C. Continue with the activity another day
D. Assign homework on the concept

54. **How could a KWL chart be used in instruction?**
(Average)

A. To motivate students to do a research paper
B. To assess prior knowledge of the students
C. To assist in teaching skills
D. To put events in sequential order

55. **Which of the following is an example of a synthesis question according to Bloom's taxonomy?**
(Rigorous)

A. "What is the definition of_____?"
B. "Compare _____ to _____."
C. "Match column A to column B."
D. "Propose an alternative to_____."

56. **Which statement is an example of specific praise?**
(Average)

A. "John, you are the only person in class not paying attention"
B. "William, I thought we agreed that you would turn in all of your homework"
C. "Robert, you did a good job staying in line. See how it helped us get to music class on time?"
D. "Class, you did a great job cleaning up the art room"

57. **Mrs. Grant is providing her students with many extrinsic motivators in order to increase their intrinsic motivation. Which of the following best explains this relationship?**
(Rigorous)

A. This is a good relationship and will increase intrinsic motivation
B. The relationship builds animosity between the teacher and the students
C. Extrinsic motivation does not in itself help to build intrinsic motivation
D. There is no place for extrinsic motivation in the classroom

58. **Which of the following is NOT a factor in student self-motivation?**
(Rigorous)

A. Breaking larger tasks into more manageable steps
B. Permitting students to turn in assignments late
C. Offering students control over the assignment
D. Allowing students to create dream boards

59. **Which of the following is NOT a part of the hardware of a computer system?**
(Easy)

A. Storage device
B. Input devices
C. Software
D. Central Processing Unit

60. **When pulling educational information from shared drives what is the MOST important factor to consider?**
(Rigorous)

A. What is the intended use of the information
B. What age group is the information best suited for
C. Where the information came from
D. Who the author of the information is

61. **Which of the following are the three primary categories of instructional technology tools?**
(Rigorous)

A. Creation/design/implementation
B. Research/implementation/assessment
C. Assessment/creation/research
D. Design/research/usage

62. **When a teacher is evaluating a student's technologically produced product, which of the following is considered the MOST important factor to consider?**
(Rigorous)

A. Content
B. Design
C. Audience
D. Relevance

63. You are a classroom teacher in a building that does not have a computer lab for your class to use. However, knowing that you enjoy incorporating technology into the classroom, your principal has worked to find computers for your room. They are set up in the back of your classroom and have software loaded, but have no access to the intranet or internet within your building. Which of the following is NOT an acceptable method for using these computers within your classroom instruction? *(Rigorous)*

A. Rotating the students in small groups through the computers as centers
B. Putting students at the computers individually for skill-based review or practice
C. Dividing your classroom into three groups and putting each group at one computer and completing a whole class lesson
D. Using the computers for students to complete their writing assignments with an assigned sign-up sheet, so the students know the order in which they will type their stories

64. What are three steps, in the correct order, for evaluating software before purchasing it for use within the classroom? *(Rigorous)*

A. Read the instructions to ensure it will work with the computer you have, try it out as if you were a student, and examine how the program handles errors or mistakes the student may make
B. Try the computer program as if you were a student, read any online information about the program, have a student use the program and provide feedback
C. Read the instructions and load it onto your computer, try out the program yourself as if you were a student, have a student use the program and provide feedback
D. Read the instructions, have a student use the program, try it out yourself

65. When a teacher wants to utilize an assessment that is subjective in nature, which of the following is the most effective method for scoring? *(Easy)*

A. Rubric
B. Checklist
C. Alternative assessment
D. Subjective measures should not be utilized

66. **What is an example of formative feedback?**
(Average)

A. The results of an intelligence test
B. Correcting the tests in small groups
C. Verbal behavior that expresses approval of a student response to a test item
D. Scheduling a discussion prior to the test

67. **Norm-referenced tests:**
(Rigorous)

A. Give information only about the local samples results
B. Provide information about how the local test takers did compared to a representative sampling of national test takers
C. Make no comparisons to national test takers
D. None of the above

68. **What is the best definition for an achievement test?**
(Average)

A. It measures mechanical and practical abilities
B. It measures broad areas of knowledge that are the result of cumulative learning experiences
C. It measures the ability to learn to perform a task
D. It measures performance related to specific, recently acquired information

69. **How are standardized tests useful in assessment?**
(Average)

A. For teacher evaluation
B. For evaluation of the administration
C. For comparison from school to school
D. For comparison to the population on which the test was normed

70. **Mr. Brown wishes to improve his parent communication skills. Which of the following is a strategy he can utilize to accomplish this goal?**
(Easy)

A. Hold parent-teacher conferences
B. Send home positive notes
C. Have parent nights where the parents are invited into his classroom
D. All of the above

71. **When communicating with parents for whom English is not the primary language, you should:**
(Easy)

A. Provide materials whenever possible in their native language
B. Use an interpreter
C. Provide the same communication as you would to native English speaking parents
D. All of the above

72. **Which statement best reflects why family involvement is important to a student's educational success?**
(Easy)

A. Reading the class newsletter constitutes strong family involvement
B. Family involvement means to attend graduation
C. There are limited ways a parent can be active in their child's education
D. The more family members are involved, the more success a student is likely to experience

73. **Which of the following is NOT an appropriate method for teachers to interact with families of diverse backgrounds?**
(Easy)

A. Show respect to parents
B. Share personal stories concerning the student
C. Display patience with parents
D. Disregard culture of student

74. **A parent has left an angry message on the teacher's voicemail. The message relates to a concern about a student and is directed at the teacher. The teacher should:**
(Average)

A. Call back immediately and confront the parent
B. Cool off, plan what to discuss with the parent, then call back
C. Question the child to find out what set off the parent
D. Ignore the message, since feelings of anger usually subside after a while

75. **Which is NOT considered a good practice when conducting parent-teacher conferences?**
(Average)

A. Ending the conference with an agreed plan of action
B. Figure out questions for parents during the conference
C. Prepare work samples, records of behavior, and assessment information
D. Prepare a welcoming environment, set a good mood, and be an active listener

76. Which of the following should NOT be a purpose of a parent-teacher conference? *(Average)*

A. To involve the parent in their child's education
B. To establish a friendship with the child's parents
C. To resolve a concern about the child's performance
D. To inform parents of positive behaviors by the child

77. Which of the following is a technological strategy that keeps students and teachers interactively communicating about issues in the classroom and beyond? *(Rigorous)*

A. Distance learning
B. Mentoring support system
C. Conceptual learning modalities
D. Community resources

78. In the past, teaching has been viewed as _____ while in more current society it has been viewed as _____. *(Rigorous)*

A. isolating…collaborative
B. collaborative…isolating
C. supportive…isolating
D. isolating…supportive

79. Which of the following is a good reason to collaborate with a peer? *(Easy)*

A. To increase your knowledge in areas where you feel you are weak, but the peer is strong
B. To increase your planning time and that of your peer by combining the classes and taking more breaks
C. To have fewer lesson plans to write
D. To teach fewer subjects

80. Which of the following is responsible for working with the school in matters concerning the business of running a school? *(Rigorous)*

A. Curriculum coordinators
B. Administrators
C. Board of Education
D. Parent-Teacher organizations

81. What would happen if a school utilized an integrated approach to professional development? *(Average)*

A. All stakeholders needs are addressed
B. Teachers and administrators are on the same page
C. High-quality programs for students are developed
D. Parents drive the curriculum and instruction

82. **Which is true of child protective services?**
(Rigorous)

A. They have been forced to become more punitive in their attempts to treat and prevent child abuse and neglect
B. They have become more a means for identifying cases of abuse and less an agent for rehabilitation due to the large volume of cases
C. They have become advocates for structured discipline within the school
D. They have become a strong advocate in the court system

83. **What is a benefit of frequent self-assessment?**
(Average)

A. Opens new venues for professional development
B. Saves teachers the pressure of being observed by others
C. Reduces time spent on areas not needing attention
D. Offers a model for students to adopt in self-improvement

84. **Mrs. Graham has taken the time to reflect, completed observations, and asked for feedback about the interactions between her and her students from her principal. It is obvious by seeking this information out that Mrs. Graham understands which of the following?**
(Rigorous)

A. The importance of clear communication with the principal
B. She needs to analyze her effectiveness of classroom interactions
C. She is clearly communicating with the principal
D. She cares about her students

85. **Which of the following are ways a professional can assess his/her teaching strengths and weaknesses?**
(Rigorous)

A. Examining how many students were unable to understand a concept
B. Asking peers for suggestions or ideas
C. Self-evaluation/reflection of lessons taught
D. All of the above

86. **In successful inclusion of students with disabilities:** *(Average)*

   A. A variety of instructional arrangements are available
   B. School personnel shift the responsibility for learning outcomes to the student
   C. The physical facilities are used as they are
   D. Regular classroom teachers have sole responsibility for evaluating student progress

87. **Teachers may duplicate copies of informational materials provided that they meet the following requirement/s:** *(Rigorous)*

   A. Brevity
   B. Spontaneity
   C. Cumulative effect
   D. All of the above

88. **Which of the following is one of the greatest obstacles that new teachers face when first entering the profession?** *(Rigorous)*

   A. Dealing with behavioral issues in the classroom
   B. Monitoring daily student success
   C. Developing rapport with parents and caretakers
   D. Creating weekly lesson plans

89. **How can a teacher use a student's permanent record?** *(Average)*

   A. To develop a better understanding of the needs of the student
   B. To record all instances of student disruptive behavior
   C. To brainstorm ideas for discussing with parents at parent-teacher conferences
   D. To develop realistic expectations of the student's performance early in the year

90. **To what does the validity of a test refer?** *(Rigorous)*

   A. Its consistency
   B. Its usefulness
   C. Its accuracy
   D. The degree of true scores it provide

Answer Key

1.	B	31.	C	61.	C
2.	C	32.	C	62.	D
3.	A	33.	D	63.	C
4.	B	34.	D	64.	A
5.	C	35.	B	65.	A
6.	B	36.	B	66.	C
7.	B	37.	D	67.	B
8.	A	38.	C	68.	B
9.	A	39.	C	69.	D
10.	D	40.	C	70.	D
11.	D	41.	A	71.	D
12.	C	42.	A	72.	D
13.	B	43.	B	73.	D
14.	C	44.	B	74.	B
15.	C	45.	B	75.	B
16.	A	46.	B	76.	B
17.	C	47.	B	77.	A
18.	B	48.	C	78.	A
19.	A	49.	C	79.	A
20.	B	50.	D	80.	C
21.	B	51.	B	81.	C
22.	C	52.	D	82.	B
23.	D	53.	A	83.	A
24.	C	54.	B	84.	B
25.	B	55.	D	85.	D
26.	A	56.	C	86.	A
27.	A	57.	C	87.	D
28.	B	58.	B	88.	A
29.	A	59.	C	89.	A
30.	B	60.	A	90.	B

Rigor Table

Easy
2, 5, 15, 22, 25, 33, 37, 47, 51, 59, 65, 70, 71, 72, 73, 79

Average
1, 4, 7, 11, 12, 13, 14, 20, 21, 26, 28, 29, 39, 40, 41, 42, 44, 49, 52, 53, 54, 56, 66, 68, 69, 74, 75, 76, 81, 83, 86, 89

Rigorous
3, 6, 8, 9, 10, 16, 17, 18, 19, 23, 24, 27, 30, 31, 32, 34, 35, 36, 38, 43, 45, 46, 48, 50, 55, 57, 58, 60, 61, 62, 63, 64, 67, 77, 78, 80, 82, 84, 85, 87, 88, 90

SAMPLE TEST WITH RATIONALES

Directions: Read each item and select the best response.

1. **What developmental patterns should a professional teacher assess to meet the needs of the student?**
   (Average)

   A. Academic, regional, and family background
   B. Social, physical, and cognitive
   C. Academic, physical, and family background
   D. Physical, family, and ethnic background

Answer: B. Social, physical, and cognitive
The effective teacher applies knowledge of physical, social, and cognitive developmental patterns and of individual differences to meet the instructional needs of all students in the classroom. The most important premise of child development is that all domains of development (physical, social, and academic) are integrated. The teacher has a broad knowledge and thorough understanding of the development that typically occurs during the students' current period of life. More importantly, the teacher understands how children learn best during each period of development. An examination of the student's file coupled with ongoing evaluation assures a successful educational experience for both teacher and students.

2. **According to Piaget, what stage is characterized by the ability to think abstractly and to use logic?**
   (Easy)

   A. Concrete operations
   B. Pre-operational
   C. Formal operations
   D. Conservative operational

Answer: C. Formal operations
The four development stages are described in Piaget's theory as follows:

1. Sensorimotor stage: from birth to age 2 years (children experience the world through movement and senses)
2. Preoperational stage: from ages 2 to 7 (acquisition of motor skills)
3. Concrete operational stage: from ages 7 to 11 (children begin to think logically about concrete events)
4. Formal operational stage: after age 11 (development of abstract reasoning)

These chronological periods are approximate and, in light of the fact that studies have demonstrated great variation between children, cannot be seem as rigid norms. Furthermore, these stages occur at different ages, depending upon the domain of knowledge under consideration. The ages normally given for the stages reflect when each stage tends to predominate even though one might elicit examples of two, three, or even all four stages of thinking at the same time from one individual, depending upon the domain of knowledge and the means used to elicit it.

3. **At approximately what age is the average child able to define abstract terms such as honesty and justice?**
   (Rigorous)

   A. 10–12 years old
   B. 4–6 years old
   C. 14–16 years old
   D. 6–8 years old

Answer: A. 10–12 years old
The usual age for the fourth stage (the formal operational stage) as described by Piaget is from 10 to 12 years old. It is in this stage that children begin to be able to define abstract terms.

4. **What would improve planning for instruction?**
   (Average)

   A. Describe the role of the teacher and student
   B. Evaluate the outcomes of instruction
   C. Rearrange the order of activities
   D. Give outside assignments

Answer: B. Evaluate the outcomes of instruction

Important as it is to plan content, materials, activities, and goals taking into account learner needs and to base what goes on in the classroom on the results of that planning, it makes no difference if students are not able to demonstrate improvement in the skills being taught. An important part of the planning process is for the teacher to constantly adapt all aspects of the curriculum to what is actually happening in the classroom. Planning frequently misses the mark or fails to allow for unexpected factors. Evaluating the outcomes of instruction regularly and making adjustments accordingly will have a positive impact on the overall success of a teaching methodology.

5. **What is the most significant development emerging in children at age two?**
   (Easy)

   A. Immune system develops
   B. Socialization occurs
   C. Language develops
   D. Perception develops

Answer: C. Language develops

Language begins to develop in an infant not long after birth. Chomsky claims that children teach themselves to speak using the people around them for resources. Several studies of the sounds infants make in their cribs seem to support this. The first stage of meaningful sounds is the uttering of a word that obviously has meaning for the child, for example "bird," when the child sees one flying through the air. Does the development of real language begin when the noun is linked with a verb ("bird fly")? When language begins and how it develops has been debated for a long time. It is useful for a teacher to investigate those theories and studies.

6.   **You are leading a substance abuse discussion for health class. The students present their belief that marijuana is not harmful to their health. What set of data would refute their claim?**
(Rigorous)

A. It is more carcinogenic than nicotine, lowers resistance to infection, worsens acne, and damages brain cells
B. It damages brain cells, causes behavior changes in prenatally exposed infants, leads to other drug abuse, and causes short-term memory loss
C. It lowers tolerance for frustration, causes eye damage, increases paranoia, and lowers resistance to infection
D. It leads to abusing alcohol, lowers white blood cell count, reduces fertility, and causes gout

Answer: B. It damages brain cells, causes behavior changes in prenatally exposed infants, leads to other drug abuse, and causes short-term memory loss
The student tending toward the use of drugs and/or alcohol will exhibit losses in social and academic functional levels that were previously attained. He may begin to experiment with substances. The adage "Pot makes a smart kid average and an average kid dumb" is right on the mark. There exist not a few families where pot smoking is a known habit of the parents. The children start their habit by stealing from the parents, making it almost impossible to convince the child that drugs and alcohol are not good for them. Parental use is hampering national efforts to clean up America. The school may be the only source for the real information that children need in order to make intelligent choices about drug use. It's important to remember that if children start using drugs early, it will interfere with their accomplishing developmental tasks and will likely lead to a lifetime of addiction.

7.   **Bobby, a nine-year-old, has been caught stealing frequently in the classroom. What might be a factor contributing to this behavior?**
     (Average)

     A. Need for the items stolen
     B. Serious emotional disturbance
     C. Desire to experiment
     D. A normal stage of development

Answer: B. Serious emotional disturbance
Lying, stealing, and fighting are atypical behaviors that most children may exhibit occasionally, but if a child lies, steals, or fights regularly or blatantly, these behaviors may be indicative of emotional distress. Emotional disturbances in childhood are not uncommon and take a variety of forms. Usually these problems show up in the form of uncharacteristic behaviors. Most of the time, children respond favorably to brief treatment programs of psychotherapy. At other times, disturbances may need more intensive therapy and are harder to resolve. All stressful behaviors need to be addressed, and any type of chronic antisocial behavior needs to be examined as a possible symptom of deep-seated emotional upset.

8.   **What strategy can teachers incorporate in their classrooms that will allow students to acquire the same academic skills even though the students are at various learning levels?**
     (Rigorous)

     A. Create learning modules
     B. Apply concrete rules to abstract theories
     C. Incorporate social learning skills
     D. Follow cognitive development progression

Answer: A. Create learning modules
Teachers should be aware of the fact that each student develops cognitively, mentally, emotionally, and physically at different levels. Each student is a unique person and may require individualized instruction. This may require teachers to adapt their lesson plans according to a student's developmental progress.

9.   The process approach is a three-phase model approach that aims directly at the enhancement of self concept among students. Which of the following are components of this process approach?
(Rigorous)

A. Sensing function, transforming function, acting function
B. Diversity model, ethnicity model, economic model
C. Problem approach, acting function, diversity model
D. Ethnicity approach, sensing model, problem approach

Answer: A. Sensing function, transforming function, acting function
This three-phase approach can be simplified into the words by which the model is usually known: reach, touch, and teach. The sensing function integrates information. The transforming function conceptualizes and provides meaning and value to perceived information. The acting function chooses actions from several different alternatives to be acted upon. This three-phase approach can be applied to any situation.

10.   Andy shows up to class abusive and irritable. He is often late, sleeps in class, sometimes slurs his speech, and has an odor of drinking. What is the first intervention to take?
(Rigorous)

A. Confront him, relying on a trusting relationship you think you have
B. Do a lesson on alcohol abuse, making an example of him
C. Do nothing, it is better to err on the side of failing to identify substance abuse
D. Call administration, avoid conflict, and supervise others carefully

Answer: D. Call administration, avoid conflict, and supervise others carefully
Educators are not only likely to, but often do, face students who are high on something. Of course, they are not only a hazard to their own safety and those of others, but their ability to be productive learners is greatly diminished, if not non-existent. They show up instead of skip, because it is not always easy or practical for them to spend the day away from home but not in school. Unless they can stay inside they are at risk of being picked up for truancy. Some enjoy being high in school, getting a sense of satisfaction by putting something over on the system. Some just do not take drug use seriously enough to think usage at school might be inappropriate. The first responsibility of the teacher is to assure the safety of all of the children. Avoiding conflict with the student who is high and obtaining help from administration is the best course of action.

11. **What is a good strategy for teaching ethnically diverse students?**
(Average)

    A. Do not focus on the students' culture
    B. Expect them to assimilate easily into your classroom
    C. Imitate their speech patterns
    D. Include ethnic studies in the curriculum

Answer: D. Include ethnic studies in the curriculum
Exploring a student's own culture increases their confidence levels in the group. It is also a very useful tool when students are struggling to develop identities that they can feel comfortable with. The bonus is that this is good training for living in the world.

12. **Which of the following is an accurate description of an English Language Learner student?**
(Average)

    A. Remedial students
    B. Exceptional education students
    C. Are not a homogeneous group
    D. Feel confident in communicating in English when with their peers

Answer: C. Are not a homogenous group
Because ELL students are often grouped in classes that take a different approach to teaching English than those for native speakers, it is easy to assume that they are all present with the same needs and characteristics. Nothing could be further from the truth, even in what they need when it comes to learning English. It is important that their backgrounds and personalities be observed just as with native speakers. It was very surprising several years ago when Vietnamese children began arriving in American schools with little training in English and went on to excel in their classes, often even beyond their American counterparts. In many schools, there were Vietnamese merit scholars in the graduating classes.

13. **What is an effective way to help an English Language Learner student succeed in class?**
(Average)

A. Refer the child to a specialist
B. Maintain an encouraging, success-oriented atmosphere
C. Help them assimilate by making them use English exclusively
D. Help them cope with the content materials you presently use

Answer: B. Maintain an encouraging, success-oriented atmosphere
Anyone who is in an environment where his language is not the standard one feels embarrassed and inferior. The student who is in that situation expects to fail. Encouragement is even more important for these students. They need many opportunities to succeed.

14. **Johnny, a middle-schooler, comes to class uncharacteristically tired, distracted, withdrawn, and sullen and cries easily. What should be the teacher's first response?**
(Average)

A. Send him to the office to sit
B. Call his parents
C. Ask him what is wrong
D. Ignore his behavior

Answer: C. Ask him what is wrong
If a teacher has developed a trusting relationship with a child, the reasons for the child's behavior may come out. It might be that the child needs to tell someone what is going on and is seeking a confidant, and a trusted teacher can intervene. If the child is unwilling to talk to the teacher about what is going on, the next step is to contact the parents, who may or may not be willing to explain why the child is the way he/she is. If they simply do not know, then it is time to add a professional physician or counselor to the mix.

15.   **What should be considered when evaluating textbooks for content? (Easy)**

   A. Type of print used
   B. Number of photographs used
   C. Free of cultural stereotyping
   D. Outlines at the beginning of each chapter

Answer: C. Free of cultural stereotyping
While textbook writers and publishers have responded to the need to be culturally diverse in recent years, a few texts are still being offered that do not meet these standards. When teachers have an opportunity to be involved in choosing textbooks, they can be watchdogs for the community in keeping the curriculum free of matter that reinforces bigotry and discrimination.

16.   **What steps are important in the review of subject matter in the classroom? (Rigorous)**

   A. A lesson-initiating review, topic, and a lesson-end review
   B. A preview of the subject matter, an in-depth discussion, and a lesson-end review
   C. A rehearsal of the subject matter and a topic summary within the lesson
   D. A short paragraph synopsis of the previous day's lesson and a written review at the end of the lesson

Answer: A. A lesson-initiating review, topic, and a lesson-end review
The effective teacher utilizes all three of these together with comprehension checks to make sure the students are processing the information. Lesson-end reviews are restatements (by the teacher or teacher and students) of the content of discussion at the end of a lesson. Subject matter retention increases when lessons include an outline at the beginning of the lesson and a summary at the end of the lesson. This type of structure is utilized in successful classrooms. Moreover, when students know what is coming next and what is expected of them, they feel more a part of their learning environment, and deviant behavior is lessened.

17. **What are critical elements of the instructional process?**
(Rigorous)

   A. Content, goals, teacher needs
   B. Means of getting money to regulate instruction
   C. Content, materials, activities, goals, learner needs
   D. Materials, definitions, assignments

Answer: C. Content, materials, activities, goals, learner needs
Goal-setting is a vital component of the instructional process. The teacher will, of course, have overall goals for her class, both short-term and long-term. However, perhaps even more important than that is the setting of goals that take into account the individual learner's needs, background, and stage of development. Making an educational program child-centered involves building on the natural curiosity children bring to school and asking children what they want to learn. Student-centered classrooms contain not only textbooks, workbooks, and literature but also rely heavily on a variety of audiovisual equipment and computers. There are tape recorders, language masters, filmstrip projectors, and laser disc players to help meet the learning styles of the students. Planning for instructional activities entails identification or selection of the activities the teacher and students will engage in during a period of instruction.

18. **The teacher states that the lesson the students will be engaged in will consist of a review of the material from the previous day, a demonstration of the scientific principles of an electronic circuit, and small group work on setting up an electronic circuit. What has the teacher demonstrated?**
(Rigorous)

   A. The importance of reviewing
   B. Giving the general framework for the lesson to facilitate learning
   C. Giving students the opportunity to leave if they are not interested in the lesson
   D. Providing momentum for the lesson

Answer: B. Giving the general framework for the lesson to facilitate learning
If children know where they're going, they're more likely to be engaged in getting there. It's important to give them a road map whenever possible for what is coming in their classes.

19. **What is one component of the instructional planning model that must be given careful evaluation?**
(Rigorous)

A. Students' prior knowledge and skills
B. The script the teacher will use in instruction
C. Future lesson plans
D. Parent participation

Answer: A. Students' prior knowledge and skills
The teacher will, of course, have certain expectations regarding where the students will be physically and intellectually when he/she plans for a new class. However, there will be wide variations in the actual classroom. If he/she does not make the extra effort to understand where there are deficiencies and where there are strengths in the individual students, the planning will probably miss the mark, at least for some members of the class. This can be obtained through a review of student records, by observation, and by testing.

20. **How many stages of intellectual development does Piaget define?**
(Average)

A. Two
B. Four
C. Six
D. Eight

Answer: B. Four
The stages are:

1. Sensorimotor stage: from birth to age 2 years (children experience the world through movement and senses)
2. Preoperational stage: from ages 2 to 7(acquisition of motor skills)
3. Concrete operational stage: from ages 7 to 11 (children begin to think logically about concrete events)
4. Formal operational stage: after age 11 (development of abstract reasoning)

21. **Who developed the theory of multiple intelligences?**
    (Average)

    A. Bruner
    B. Gardner
    C. Kagan
    D. Cooper

Answer: B. Gardner
Howard Gardner's most famous work is probably *Frames of Mind*, which details seven dimensions of intelligence (visual/spatial intelligence, musical intelligence, verbal intelligence, logical/mathematical intelligence, interpersonal intelligence, intrapersonal intelligence, and bodily/kinesthetic intelligence). Gardner's claim that pencil and paper IQ tests do not capture the full range of human intelligences has garnered much praise within the field of education but has also met criticism, largely from psychometricians. Since the publication of *Frames of Mind*, Gardner has additionally identified the 8th dimension of intelligence: naturalist intelligence, and is still considering a possible ninth—existentialist intelligence.

22. **What is an example of a low order question?**
    (Easy)

    A. "Why is it important to recycle items in your home?"
    B. "Compare how glass and plastics are recycled"
    C. "What items do we recycle in our county?"
    D. "Explain the importance of recycling in our county"

Answer: C. "What items do we recycle in our county?"
Remember that the difference between specificity and abstractness is a continuum. The most specific is something that is concrete and can be seen, heard, smelled, tasted, or felt, like cans, bottles, and newspapers. At the other end of the spectrum is an abstraction like importance. Lower-order questions are on the concrete end of the continuum; higher-order questions are on the abstract end.

23. **Bloom's taxonomy references six skill levels within the cognitive domain. The top three skills are known as higher-order thinking skills (HOTS). Which of the following are the three highest order skills?**
(Rigorous)

A. Comprehension, application, analysis
B. Knowledge, comprehension, evaluation
C. Application, synthesis, comprehension
D. Analysis, synthesis, and evaluation

Answer: D. Analysis, synthesis, and evaluation
The six skill levels of Bloom's taxonomy are: knowledge, comprehension, application, analysis, synthesis, and evaluation. Key instructional approaches that utilize HOTS are inquiry-based learning, problem solving, and open-ended questioning. It is crucial for students to use and refine these skills in order to apply them to everyday life and situations outside of school.

24. **Teachers have a responsibility to help students learn how to organize their classroom environments. Which of the following is NOT an effective method of teaching responsibility to students?**
(Rigorous)

A. Dividing responsibilities among students
B. Doing "spot-checks" of notebooks
C. Cleaning up after students leave the classroom
D. Expecting students to keep weekly calendars

Answer: C. Cleaning up after students leave the classroom
Teachers of young children can help students learn how to behave appropriately and take care of their surroundings by providing them with opportunities to practice ownership, chores, and leadership. Allowing students to leave a messy and disorganized class at the end of the day does not teach them responsibility.

25. **How can students use a computer desktop publishing center?**
    (Easy)

    A. To set up a classroom budget
    B. To create student made books, reports, essays, and more
    C. To design a research project
    D. To create a classroom behavior management system

Answer: B. To create student made books, reports, essays, and more
By creating a book, students gain new insights into how communication works. Suddenly, the concept of audience for what they write and create becomes real. They also have an opportunity to be introduced to graphic arts, an exploding field. In addition, just as computers are a vital part of the world they will be entering as adults, so is desktop publishing. It is universally used by businesses of all kinds.

26. **Which of the following is considered a study skill?**
    (Average)

    A. Using graphs, tables, and maps
    B. Using a desktop publishing program
    C. Explaining important vocabulary words
    D. Asking for clarification

Answer: A. Using graphs, tables, and maps
In studying, it is certainly true that "a picture is worth a thousand words." Not only are these devices useful in making a point clear, they are excellent mnemonic devices for remembering facts.

27. **According to research, what can be a result of specific teacher actions on behavior?**
    (Rigorous)

    A. Increase in student misconduct
    B. Increase in the number of referrals
    C. Decrease in student participation
    D. Decrease in student retentions

Answer: A. Increase in student misconduct
Unfortunately, at times, misbehavior is the result of specific teacher actions. There is considerable research that indicates that some teacher behavior is upsetting to students and increases the occurrence of student misbehavior. Such teacher behavior may include any action that a child perceives as being unfair; punitive remarks about the child, his behavior, or his work; or harsh responses to the child.

28. **When using a kinesthetic approach, what would be an appropriate activity?**
(Average)

    A. List
    B. Match
    C. Define
    D. Debate

Answer: B. Match
Brain lateralization theory emerged in the 1970s and demonstrated that the left hemisphere appeared to be associated with verbal and sequential abilities whereas the right hemisphere appeared to be associated with emotions and with spatial, holistic processing. Although those particular conclusions continue to be challenged, it is clear that people concentrate, process, and remember new and difficult information under very different conditions. For example, auditory and visual perceptual strengths, passivity, and self-oriented or authority-oriented motivation often correlate with high academic achievement, whereas tactual and kinesthetic strengths, a need for mobility, nonconformity, and peer motivation often correlate with school underachievement (Dunn & Dunn, 1992, 1993). Understanding how students perceive the task of learning new information differently is often helpful in tailoring the classroom experience for optimal success.

29. **How can the teacher establish a positive climate in the classroom?**
(Average)

    A. Help students see the unique contributions of individual differences
    B. Use whole group instruction for all content areas
    C. Help students divide into cooperative groups based on ability
    D. Eliminate teaching strategies that allow students to make choices

Answer: A. Help students see the unique contributions of individual differences
In the first place, an important purpose of education is to prepare students to live successfully in the real world, and this is an important insight and understanding for them to take into that world. In the second place, the most fertile learning environment is one in which all viewpoints and backgrounds are respected and where everyone has equal respect.

30. **How can the teacher help students become more work-oriented and less disruptive?**
(*Rigorous*)

    A. Seek their input for content instruction
    B. Challenge the students with a task and show genuine enthusiasm for it
    C. Use behavior modification techniques with all students
    D. Make sure lesson plans are complete for the week

Answer: B. Challenge the students with a task and show genuine enthusiasm for it
Many studies have demonstrated that the enthusiasm of the teacher is infectious. If students feel that the teacher is ambivalent about a task, they will also catch that attitude.

31. **What has been established to increase student originality, intrinsic motivation, and higher-order thinking skills?**
(*Rigorous*)

    A. Classroom climate
    B. High expectations
    C. Student choice
    D. Use of authentic learning opportunities

Answer: C. Student choice
While all of the descriptors are good attributes for students to demonstrate, it has been shown through research that providing student choice can increase all of the described factors.

32. **Which of the following is NOT a component of the invitational learning theory?**
(*Rigorous*)

    A. Proper arrangement of classroom furniture
    B. Adequate ventilation and classroom lighting
    C. The regular use of substitute teachers
    D. Neutral hues for coloration of walls

Answer: C. The regular use of substitute teachers
The physical environment is one of the main principles of the invitational learning theory. The teacher can create and design their classroom to cultivate a warm and caring environment for their students. This thoughtful atmosphere can create positive learning experiences for their students.

33. How can student misconduct be redirected at times?
(Easy)

    A. The teacher threatens the students
    B. The teacher assigns detention to the whole class
    C. The teacher stops the activity and stares at the students
    D. The teacher effectively handles changing from one activity to another

Answer: D. The teacher effectively handles changing from one activity to another
Appropriate verbal techniques include a soft non-threatening voice void of undue roughness, anger, or impatience regardless of whether the teacher is instructing, providing student alerts, or giving a behavior reprimand. Verbal techniques that may be effective in modifying student behavior include simply stating the student's name, explaining briefly and succinctly what the student is doing that is inappropriate and what the student should be doing. Verbal techniques for reinforcing behavior include both encouragement and praise delivered by the teacher. In addition, for verbal techniques to positively affect student behavior and learning, the teacher must give clear, concise directives while implying her warmth toward the students.

34. The concept of efficient use of time includes which of the following?
(Rigorous)

    A. Daily review, seatwork, and recitation of concepts
    B. Lesson initiation, transition, and comprehension check
    C. Review, test, and review
    D. Punctuality, management transition, and wait time avoidance

Answer: D. Punctuality, management transition, and wait time avoidance
The "benevolent boss" concept applies here. One who succeeds in managing a business follows these rules; so does the successful teacher.

35. **Reducing off-task time and maximizing the amount of time students spend attending to academic tasks is closely related to which of the following?**
(Rigorous)

    A. Using whole class instruction only
    B. Business-like behaviors of the teacher
    C. Dealing only with major teaching functions
    D. Giving students a maximum of two minutes to come to order

Answer: B. Business-like behaviors of the teacher
The effective teacher continually evaluates his/her own physical/mental/social/emotional well-being with regard to the students in his/her classroom. There is always the tendency to satisfy social and emotional needs through relationships with the students. A good teacher genuinely likes his/her students, and that is a positive thing. However, if students are not convinced that the teacher's purpose for being there is to get a job done, the atmosphere in the classroom becomes difficult to control. This is the job of the teacher. Maintaining a business-like approach in the classroom yields many positive results. It is a little like a benevolent boss.

36. **What do cooperative learning methods all have in common?**
(Rigorous)

    A. Philosophy
    B. Cooperative task/cooperative reward structures
    C. Student roles and communication
    D. Teacher roles

Answer: B. Cooperative task/cooperative reward structures
Cooperative learning situations, as practiced in today's classrooms, grew out of searches conducted by several groups in the early 1970s. Cooperative learning situations can range from very formal applications such as STAD (Student Teams-Achievement Divisions) and CIRC (Cooperative Integrated Reading and Composition) to less formal groupings known variously as "group investigation," "learning together," and "discovery groups." Cooperative learning as a general term is now firmly recognized and established as a teaching and learning technique in American schools. Since cooperative learning techniques are so widely diffused in the schools, it is necessary to orient students in the skills by which cooperative learning groups can operate smoothly, and thereby enhance learning. Students who cannot interact constructively with other students will not be able to take advantage of the learning opportunities provided by the cooperative learning situations and will furthermore deprive their fellow students of the opportunity for cooperative learning.

37. **The use of volunteers and paraprofessionals within a classroom enriches the setting by:**
(Easy)

A. Providing more opportunity for individual student attention
B. Offering a perceived sense of increased security for students
C. Modifying the behavior of students
D. All of the above

Answer: D. All of the above
Research has shown that volunteers and paraprofessionals involvement in the educational process positively impacts the attitude and conduct of children in the classroom. Always be cautious in choosing classroom helpers that you trust and are competent.

38. **What is the definition of proactive classroom management?**
(Rigorous)

A. Management that is constantly changing
B. Management that is downplayed
C. Management that gives clear and explicit instructions and rewards compliance
D. Management that is designed by the students

Answer: C. Management that gives clear and explicit instructions and rewards compliance
Classroom management plans should be in place when the school year begins. Developing a management plan takes a proactive approach—that is, decide what behaviors will be expected of the class as a whole, anticipate possible problems, and teach the behaviors early in the school year. Involving the students in the development of the classroom rules lets the students know the rationale for the rules and allows them to assume responsibility in the rules because they had a part in developing them.

39. **Which of the following significantly increases appropriate behavior in the classroom?**
(Average)

A. Monitoring the halls
B. Having class rules
C. Having class rules, giving feedback, and having individual consequences
D. Having class rules, and giving feedback

Answer: C. Having class rules, giving feedback, and having individual consequences
Clear, consistent class rules go a long way to preventing inappropriate behavior. Effective teachers give immediate feedback to students regarding their behavior or misbehavior. If there are consequences, they should be as close as possible to the outside world, especially for adolescents. Consistency, especially with adolescents, reduces the occurrence of power struggles and teaches them that predictable consequences follow for their choice of actions.

40. **What have recent studies regarding effective teachers concluded?**
(Average)

A. Effective teachers let students establish rules
B. Effective teachers establish routines by the sixth week of school
C. Effective teachers state their own policies and establish consistent class rules and procedures on the first day of class
D. Effective teachers establish flexible routines

Answer: C. Effective teachers state their own policies and establish consistent class rules and procedures on the first day of class
The teacher can get ahead of the game by stating clearly on the first day of school in her introductory information for the students exactly what the rules are. These should be stated firmly but unemotionally. When one of those rules is broken, he/she can then refer to the rules, rendering enforcement much easier to achieve. It is extremely difficult to achieve goals with students who are out of control. Establishing limits early and consistently enforcing them enhances learning. It is also helpful for the teacher to display prominently the classroom rules. This will serve as a visual reminder of the students' expected behaviors. In a study of classroom management procedures, it was established that the combination of conspicuously displayed rules, frequent verbal references to the rules, and appropriate consequences for appropriate behaviors led to increased levels of on-task behavior.

41. **What is one way of effectively managing student conduct?**
(Average)

A. State expectations about behavior
B. Let students discipline their peers
C. Let minor infractions of the rules go unnoticed
D. Increase disapproving remarks

Answer: A. State expectations about behavior
The effective teacher demonstrates awareness of what the entire class is doing and is in control of the behavior of all students even when the teacher is working with only a small group of the children. In an attempt to prevent student misbehaviors the teacher makes clear, concise statements about what is happening in the classroom directing attention to content and the students' accountability for their work rather than focusing the class on the misbehavior. It is also effective for the teacher to make a positive statement about the appropriate behavior that is observed. If deviant behavior does occur, the effective teacher will specify who the deviant is, what he or she is doing wrong, and why this is unacceptable conduct or what the proper conduct would be. This can be a difficult task to accomplish as the teacher must maintain academic focus and flow while addressing and desisting misbehavior. The teacher must make clear, brief statements about the expectations without raising his/her voice and without disrupting instruction.

42. **When is utilization of instructional materials most effective?**
(Average)

A. When the activities are organized and sequenced
B. When the materials are prepared weeks in advance
C. When the students choose the pages to work on
D. When the students create the instructional materials

Answer: A. When the activities are organized and sequenced
Most assignments will require more than one educational principle. It is helpful to explain to students the proper order in which these principles must be applied to complete the assignment successfully. Subsequently, students should also be informed of the nature of the assignment (i.e., cooperative learning, group project, individual assignment, etc). This is often done at the start of the assignment.

43. **Why is it important for a teacher to pose a question before calling on students to answer?**
   (Rigorous)

   A. It helps manage student conduct
   B. It keeps the students as a group focused on the class work
   C. It allows students time to collaborate
   D. It gives the teacher time to walk among the students

Answer: B. It keeps the students as a group focused on the class work
It does not take much distraction for a class's attention to become diffused. Once this happens, effectively teaching a principle or a skill is very difficult. The teacher should plan presentations that will keep students focused on the lesson. A very useful tool is effective, well thought-out, pointed questions.

44. **Wait-time has what effect?**
   (Average)

   A. Gives structure to the class discourse
   B. Fewer chain and low-level questions are asked with more high-level questions included
   C. Gives the students time to evaluate the response
   D. Gives the opportunity for in-depth discussion about the topic

Answer: B. Fewer chain and low-level questions are asked with more high-level questions included
One part of the questioning process for the successful teacher is *wait-time*: the time between the question and either the student response or a follow-up. Many teachers vaguely recommend some general amount of wait-time (until the student starts to get uncomfortable or is clearly perplexed), but here the focus is on wait-time as a specific and powerful communicative tool that speaks through its structured silences. Embedded in wait-time are subtle clues about judgments of a student's abilities and expectations of individuals and groups. For example, the more time a student is allowed to mull through a question, the more the teacher trusts his or her ability to answer that question without getting flustered. As a rule, the practice of prompting is not a problem. Giving support and helping students reason through difficult conundrums is part of being an effective teacher.

45. **What is one benefit of amplifying a student's response?**
(Rigorous)

    A. It helps the student develop a positive self-image
    B. It is helpful to other students who are in the process of learning the reasoning or steps in answering the question
    C. It allows the teacher to cover more content
    D. It helps to keep the information organized

Answer: B. It is helpful to other students who are in the process of learning the reasoning or steps in answering the question

Not only does the teacher show acceptance and give value to student responses by acknowledging, amplifying, discussing, or restating the comment or question, she also helps the rest of the class learn to reason. If a student response is allowed, even if it is blurted out, it must be acknowledged and the student made aware of the quality of the response. A teacher acknowledges a student response by commenting on it. For example, the teacher states the definition of a noun, and then asks for examples of nouns in the classroom. A student responds, "My pencil is a noun." The teacher answers, "Okay, let us list that on the board." By this response and the action of writing "pencil" on the board, the teacher has just incorporated the student's response into the lesson.

46. **What is not a way that teachers show acceptance and give value to a student response?**
(Rigorous)

    A. Acknowledging
    B. Correcting
    C. Discussing
    D. Amplifying

Answer: B. Correcting

There are ways to treat every answer as worthwhile even if it happens to be wrong. The objective is to keep students involved in the dialogue. If their efforts to participate are "rewarded" with what seems to them to be a rebuke or that leads to embarrassment, they will be less willing to respond the next time.

47.   **What is an effective amount of wait-time?**
       (Easy)

       A. 1 second
       B. 5 seconds
       C. 15 seconds
       D. 10 seconds

Answer: B. 5 seconds
See rationale for question 44.

48.   **Ms. Smith says, "Yes, exactly what do you mean by 'It was the author's intention to mislead you'" What does this illustrate?**
       (Rigorous)

       A. Digression
       B. Restates response
       C. Probes a response
       D. Amplifies a response

Answer: C. Probes a response
From ancient times, notable teachers such as Socrates have employed oral-questioning to enhance their discourse, to stimulate thinking, and/or to stir emotion among their audiences. Educational researchers and practitioners virtually all agree that teachers' effective use of questioning promotes student learning. Effective teachers continually develop their questioning skills.

49.   **The teacher responds, "Yes, that is correct" to a student's answer. What is this an example of?**
       (Average)

       A. Academic feedback
       B. Academic praise
       C. Simple positive response
       D. Simple negative response

Answer: C. Simple positive response
The reason for praise in the classroom is to increase the desirable in order to eliminate the undesirable. This refers to both conduct and academic focus. It further states that effective praise should be authentic, it should be used in a variety of ways, and it should be low-keyed. Academic praise is a group of specific statements that give information about the value of the response or its implications. For example, a teacher using academic praise would respond, "That is an excellent analysis of Twain's use of the river in Huckleberry Finn." Whereas a simple positive response to the same question would be, "That's correct."

50. **When are students more likely to understand complex ideas?**
    (Rigorous)

    A. If they do outside research before coming to class
    B. Later when they write out the definitions of complex words
    C. When they attend a lecture on the subject
    D. When they are clearly defined by the teacher and are given examples and non-examples of the concept

Answer: D. When they are clearly defined by the teacher and are given examples and non-examples of the concept
Several studies have been carried out to determine the effectiveness of giving examples as well as the difference in effectiveness of various types of examples. It was found conclusively that the most effective method of concept presentation included giving a definition along with examples and non-examples and also providing an explanation of them. These same studies indicate that boring examples were just as effective as interesting examples in promoting learning. Additional studies have been conducted to determine the most effective number of examples that will result in maximum student learning. These studies concluded that a few thoughtfully selected examples are just as effective as many examples. It was determined that the actual number of examples necessary to promote student learning was relative to the learning characteristics of the learners. It was again ascertained that learning is facilitated when examples are provided along with the definition.

51. **What are the two ways concepts can be taught?**
    (Easy)

    A. Factually and interpretively
    B. Inductively and deductively
    C. Conceptually and inductively
    D. Analytically and facilitatively

Answer: B. Inductively and deductively
Induction is reasoning from the particular to the general—that is, looking at a feature that exists in several examples and drawing a conclusion about that feature. Deduction is the reverse; it is the statement of the generality and then supporting it with specific examples.

52. **According to Piaget, when does the development of symbolic functioning and language take place?**
(Average)

    A. Concrete operations stage
    B. Formal operations stage
    C. Sensorimotor stage
    D. Preoperational stage

Answer: D. Preoperational stage
Although there is no general theory of cognitive development, the most historically influential theory was developed by Jean Piaget, a Swiss psychologist (1896-1980). His theory provided many central concepts in the field of developmental psychology. His theory concerned the growth of intelligence, which for Piaget meant the ability to more accurately represent the world and perform logical operations on representations of concepts grounded in the world. His theory concerns the emergence and acquisition of schemata - schemes of how one perceives the world - in "developmental stages," times when children are acquiring new ways of mentally representing information.

His theory is considered "constructivist," meaning that, unlike nativist theories (which describe cognitive development as the unfolding of innate knowledge and abilities) or empiricist theories (which describe cognitive development as the gradual acquisition of knowledge through experience), asserts that we construct our cognitive abilities through self-motivated action in the world. For his development of the theory, Piaget was awarded the Erasmus Prize.

53. **What should a teacher do when students have not responded well to an instructional activity?**
(Average)

  A. Reevaluate learner needs
  B. Request administrative help
  C. Continue with the activity another day
  D. Assign homework on the concept

Answer: A. Reevaluate learner needs
The value of teacher observations cannot be underestimated. It is through the use of observations that the teacher is able to informally assess the needs of the students during instruction. These observations will drive the lesson and determine the direction that the lesson will take based on student activity and behavior. After a lesson is carefully planned, teacher observation is the single most important component of an instructional presentation. If the teacher observes that a particular student is not on task, she will change the method of instruction accordingly. She may change from a teacher-directed approach to a more interactive approach. Questioning will increase in order to increase the participation of the students. If appropriate, the teacher will introduce manipulative materials to the lesson. In addition, teachers may switch to a cooperative group activity, thereby removing the responsibility of instruction from the teacher and putting it on the students.

54. **How could a KWL chart be used in instruction?**
(Average)

  A. To motivate students to do a research paper
  B. To assess prior knowledge of the students
  C. To assist in teaching skills
  D. To put events in sequential order

Answer: B. To assess prior knowledge of the students
To understand information, not simply repeat it, students must connect it to their previous understanding. Textbooks cannot do that. Instead, teachers—the people who know students best—have to find out what they know and how to build on that knowledge. In science, having students make predictions before conducting experiments is an obvious way of finding out what they know and having them compare their observations to those predictions helps connect new knowledge and old. In history, teachers can also ask students what they know about a topic before they begin studying it or ask them to make predictions about what they will learn. KWL charts, in which students discuss what they know, what they want to know, and (later), what they have learned, are one way to activate this prior knowledge.

55. **Which of the following is an example of a synthesis question according to Bloom's taxonomy?**
    (Rigorous)

    A. "What is the definition of_____?"
    B. "Compare ____ to ____."
    C. "Match column A to column   B."
    D. "Propose an alternative to_____."

Answer: D. "Propose an alternative to_____"
There are six levels to the taxonomy: knowledge, comprehension, application, analysis, synthesis, and evaluation. Synthesis is compiling information together in a different way by combining elements in a new pattern or proposing alternative solutions to produce a unique communication, plan, or proposed set of operations or to derive a set of abstract relations.

56. **Which statement is an example of specific praise?**
    (Average)

    A. "John, you are the only person in class not paying attention"
    B. "William, I thought we agreed that you would turn in all of your homework"
    C. "Robert, you did a good job staying in line. See how it helped us get to music class on time?"
    D. "Class, you did a great job cleaning up the art room"

Answer: C. "Robert, you did a good job staying in line. See how it helped us get to music class on time?"
Praise is a powerful tool in obtaining and maintaining order in a classroom. In addition, it is an effective motivator. It is even more effective if the positive results of good behavior are included.

57. **Mrs. Grant is providing her students with many extrinsic motivators in order to increase their intrinsic motivation. Which of the following best explains this relationship?**
     (Rigorous)

     A. This is a good relationship and will increase intrinsic motivation
     B. The relationship builds animosity between the teacher and the students
     C. Extrinsic motivation does not in itself help to build intrinsic motivation
     D. There is no place for extrinsic motivation in the classroom

Answer: C. Extrinsic motivation does not in itself help to build intrinsic motivation
There are some cases where it is necessary to utilize extrinsic motivation; however, the use of extrinsic motivation is not alone a strategy to use to build intrinsic motivation. Intrinsic motivation comes from within the student themselves, while extrinsic motivation comes from outside parties.

58. **Which of the following is NOT a factor in student self-motivation?**
     (Rigorous)

     A. Breaking larger tasks into more manageable steps
     B. Permitting students to turn in assignments late
     C. Offering students control over the assignment
     D. Allowing students to create dream boards

Answer: B. Permitting students to turn in assignments late
Student motivation in the classroom is an essential component of teaching. Highly motivated students actively engage more in the learning process than less motivated students. Teachers should have a firm understanding of the diverse aspects that influence student motivation and then incorporate strategies for encouraging motivation in the classroom.

59. **Which of the following is NOT a part of the hardware of a computer system?**
     (Easy)

     A. Storage device
     B. Input devices
     C. Software
     D. Central Processing Unit

Answer: C. Software
Software is not a part of the hardware of a computer but instead consists of all of the programs which allow the computer to run. Software is either an operating system or an application program.

60. **When pulling educational information from shared drives what is the MOST important factor to consider?**
(Rigorous)

   A. What is the intended use of the information
   B. What age group is the information best suited for
   C. Where the information came from
   D. Who the author of the information is

Answer: A. What is the intended use of the information
The concept of using shared drives is well established and as with most educational network operating systems, retrieving information is relatively straightforward. However, it is fundamentally important to know that not all information is the best suited for classroom instruction. Each lesson will need to be tailored and adjusted to students' needs.

61. **Which of the following are the three primary categories of instructional technology tools?**
(Rigorous)

   A. Creation/design/implementation
   B. Research/implementation/assessment
   C. Assessment/creation/research
   D. Design/research/usage

Answer: C. Assessment/creation/research
Assessment programs may not necessarily teach students about technology but are very clear-cut and simple programs to use. Creation is the category where students can practice their technology skills. Teachers can permit students to utilize their researching skills by allowing classroom time to research the topics they are studying. This also allows them to keep them abreast of technological advances.

62. **When a teacher is evaluating a student's technologically produced product, which of the following is considered the MOST important factor to consider?**
    (Rigorous)

    A. Content
    B. Design
    C. Audience
    D. Relevance

Answer: D. Relevance
All of the above are important; however, relevance is of utmost importance. It is imperative that students are aware of how to design a technologically based assignment and also to incorporate effective content. However, if the content is not relevant and pertinent to the topic studied, it is not considered an effective learning strategy.

63. **You are a classroom teacher in a building that does not have a computer lab for your class to use. However, knowing that you enjoy incorporating technology into the classroom, your principal has worked to find computers for your room. They are set up in the back of your classroom and have software loaded, but have no access to the intranet or internet within your building. Which of the following is NOT an acceptable method for using these computers within your classroom instruction?**
    (Rigorous)

    A. Rotating the students in small groups through the computers as centers
    B. Putting students at the computers individually for skill-based review or practice
    C. Dividing your classroom into three groups and putting each group at one computer and completing a whole class lesson
    D. Using the computers for students to complete their writing assignments with an assigned sign-up sheet, so the students know the order in which they will type their stories

Answer: C. Dividing your classroom into three groups and putting each group at one computer and completing a whole class lesson
Three computers are not enough for a typical class size across the country. This would involve too many students at one computer and could result in behavioral issues. Additionally, it would be difficult for the students to all have the ability to interact in a meaningful way with the software. If you would like to complete a whole class lesson using the technology, it would be best to find a projector that connects to the computer so all students have equal opportunity to participate and see.

64. **What are three steps, in the correct order, for evaluating software before purchasing it for use within the classroom?**
(Rigorous)

   A. Read the instructions to ensure it will work with the computer you have, try it out as if you were a student, and examine how the program handles errors or mistakes the student may make
   B. Try the computer program as if you were a student, read any online information about the program, have a student use the program and provide feedback
   C. Read the instructions and load it onto your computer, try out the program yourself as if you were a student, have a student use the program and provide feedback
   D. Read the instructions, have a student use the program, try it out yourself

Answer: A. Read the instructions to ensure it will work with the computer you have, try it out as if you were a student, and examine how the program handles errors or mistakes the students may make
You should not have students use the program until you have read all of the material related to the use, tried it out yourself as if you were a student and made many different types of mistakes when using it. You should try to make as many different types of errors as possible, so that you can see how the program responds and ensure it is how you want your student's errors handled.

65. **When a teacher wants to utilize an assessment that is subjective in nature, which of the following is the most effective method for scoring?**
(Easy)

   A. Rubric
   B. Checklist
   C. Alternative assessment
   D. Subjective measures should not be utilized

Answer: A. Rubric
Rubrics are the most effective tool for assessing items that can be considered subjective. They provide the students with a clearer picture of teacher expectations and provide the teacher with a more consistent method of comparing this type of assignment.

66. **What is an example of formative feedback?**
(Average)

   A. The results of an intelligence test
   B. Correcting the tests in small groups
   C. Verbal behavior that expresses approval of a student response to a test item
   D. Scheduling a discussion prior to the test

Answer: C. Verbal behavior that expresses approval of a student response to a test item
Standardized testing is currently under great scrutiny, but educators agree that any test that serves as a means of gathering and interpreting information about children's learning and that can provide accurate, helpful input for nurturing children's further growth is acceptable. All testing must be formative in nature. Formative evaluation is the basic, everyday kind of assessment that teachers continually do to understand students' growth and to help them learn further.

67. **Norm-referenced tests:**
(Rigorous)

   A. Give information only about the local samples results
   B. Provide information about how the local test takers did compared to a representative sampling of national test takers
   C. Make no comparisons to national test takers
   D. None of the above

Answer: B. Provide information about how the local test takers did compared to a representative sampling of national test takers
This is the definition of a norm-referenced test.

68. **What is the best definition for an achievement test?**
(Average)

   A. It measures mechanical and practical abilities
   B. It measures broad areas of knowledge that are the result of cumulative learning experiences
   C. It measures the ability to learn to perform a task
   D. It measures performance related to specific, recently acquired information

Answer: B. It measures broad areas of knowledge that are the result of cumulative learning experiences
The ways that a teacher uses test data is a meaningful aspect of instruction and may increase the motivation level of the students especially when this information is available in the form of feedback to the students. This feedback should indicate to the students what they need to do in order to improve their achievement. Frequent testing and feedback is most often an effective way to increase achievement.

69. **How are standardized tests useful in assessment?**
(Average)

A. For teacher evaluation
B. For evaluation of the administration
C. For comparison from school to school
D. For comparison to the population on which the test was normed

Answer: D. For comparison to the population on which the test was normed
While the efficacy of the standardized tests that are being used nationally has come under attack recently, they are actually the only device for comparing where an individual student stands with a wide range of peers. They also provide a measure for a program or a school to evaluate how their own students are doing as compared to the populace at large.

70. **Mr. Brown wishes to improve his parent communication skills. Which of the following is a strategy he can utilize to accomplish this goal?**
(Easy)

A. Hold parent-teacher conferences
B. Send home positive notes
C. Have parent nights where the parents are invited into his classroom
D. All of the above

Answer: D. All of the above
Increasing parent communication skills is important for teachers. All of the listed strategies are methods a teacher can utilize to increase his skills.

71. **When communicating with parents for whom English is not the primary language, you should:**
(Easy)

A. Provide materials whenever possible in their native language
B. Use an interpreter
C. Provide the same communication as you would to native English speaking parents
D. All of the above

Answer: D. All of the above
When communicating with non-English speaking parents, it is important to treat them as you would any other parent and utilize any means necessary to ensure they have the ability to participate in their child's educational process.

72. **Which statement best reflects why family involvement is important to a student's educational success?**
    (Easy)

    A. Reading the class newsletter constitutes strong family involvement
    B. Family involvement means to attend graduation
    C. There are limited ways a parent can be active in their child's education
    D. The more family members are involved, the more success a student is likely to experience

Answer: D. The more family members are involved, the more success a student is likely to experience
Although reading the class newsletter and coming to graduation are obvious parts of parental involvement, it is not the sole involvement for which teachers hope. Unlike the statement in choice C, there are many unique ways parents can participate and share talents toward their child's education. Parents are invited in to assist with workshops, attend class trips, participate as room parents, organize special events, read to the class, speak of an occupation, help with classroom housekeeping, and more. Parents can also be involved by volunteering for the PTO/A, library help, office help, and other tasks. Some teachers plan a few events a year in the classroom for special parties, presentations and events.

73. **Which of the following is NOT an appropriate method for teachers to interact with families of diverse backgrounds?**
    (Easy)

    A. Show respect to parents
    B. Share personal stories concerning the student
    C. Display patience with parents
    D. Disregard culture of student

Answer: D. Disregard culture of student
The culture of the student must be taken into account when interacting with families of diverse backgrounds. Teachers must show respect to all parents and families, and they need to realize that various cultures have different views of how children should be educated—this must be taken into consideration when dealing with families.

74. **A parent has left an angry message on the teacher's voicemail. The message relates to a concern about a student and is directed at the teacher. The teacher should:**
(Average)

A. Call back immediately and confront the parent
B. Cool off, plan what to discuss with the parent, then call back
C. Question the child to find out what set off the parent
D. Ignore the message, since feelings of anger usually subside after a while

Answer: B. Cool off, plan what to discuss with the parent, then call back
It is professional for a teacher to keep her head in the face of emotion and respond to an angry parent in a calm and objective manner. The teacher should give herself time to cool off and plan the conversation with the parents with the purpose of understanding the concern and resolving it, rather than putting the parent in his or her place. Above all, the teacher should remember that parent-teacher interactions should aim to benefit the student.

75. **Which is NOT considered a good practice when conducting parent-teacher conferences?**
(Average)

A. Ending the conference with an agreed plan of action
B. Figure out questions for parents during the conference
C. Prepare work samples, records of behavior, and assessment information
D. Prepare a welcoming environment, set a good mood, and be an active listener

Answer: B. Figure out questions for parents during the conference
Choices A, C, and D all reflect effective practices for holding a successful parent teacher conference. Teachers should prepare questions and comments for parents prior to the conference so they are optimally prepared.

76. **Which of the following should NOT be a purpose of a parent-teacher conference?**
   (Average)

   A. To involve the parent in their child's education
   B. To establish a friendship with the child's parents
   C. To resolve a concern about the child's performance
   D. To inform parents of positive behaviors by the child

Answer: B. To establish a friendship with the child's parents
The purpose of a parent-teacher conference is to involve parents in their child's education, address concerns about the child's performance, and share positive aspects of the student's learning with the parents. It would be unprofessional to allow the conference to degenerate into a social visit to establish a friendship.

77. **Which of the following is a technological strategy that keeps students and teachers interactively communicating about issues in the classroom and beyond?**
   (Rigorous)

   A. Distance learning
   B. Mentoring support system
   C. Conceptual learning modalities
   D. Community resources

Answer: A. Distance learning
Distance learning is the process of creating educational experiences for students outside the classroom. This growing technological tool is becoming widely used in schools and institutions around the country. With the recent trend of technological advances, distance learning is becoming highly appreciated as an effective learning strategy.

78. **In the past, teaching has been viewed as _____ while in more current society it has been viewed as _____.**
   (Rigorous)

   A. isolating…collaborative
   B. collaborative…isolating
   C. supportive…isolating
   D. isolating…supportive

Answer: A. isolating…collaborative
In the past, teachers often walked into their own classrooms and closed the door. They were not involved in any form of collaboration and were responsible for only the students within their classrooms. However, in today's more modern schools, teachers work in collaborative teams and are responsible for all of the children in a school setting.

79. **Which of the following is a good reason to collaborate with a peer?**
(Easy)

   A. To increase your knowledge in areas where you feel you are weak, but the peer is strong
   B. To increase your planning time and that of your peer by combining the classes and taking more breaks
   C. To have fewer lesson plans to write
   D. To teach fewer subjects

Answer: A. To increase your knowledge in areas where you feel you are weak, but the peer is strong
One of the best reasons to collaborate is to share and develop your knowledge base.

80. **Which of the following is responsible for working with the school in matters concerning the business of running a school?**
(Rigorous)

   A. Curriculum coordinators
   B. Administrators
   C. Board of Education
   D. Parent-Teacher organizations

Answer: C. Board of Education
The Board of Education is elected by the district to offer direction for the students and their schools. Among its many responsibilities, the Board establishes a long-term vision for the district and designs their policies and goals. The administrator carries out the school district's policies and manages the day-to-day operations of the school.

81. **What would happen if a school utilized an integrated approach to professional development?**
(Average)

   A. All stakeholders needs are addressed
   B. Teachers and administrators are on the same page
   C. High-quality programs for students are developed
   D. Parents drive the curriculum and instruction

Answer: C. High-quality programs for students are developed
The implementation of an integrated approach to professional development is a critical component to ensuring success of programs for students. It involves teachers, parents, and other community members working together to develop appropriate programs to ensure students are receiving the necessary instruction to be successful in the future workforce.

82. **Which is true of child protective services?**
    (Rigorous)

    A. They have been forced to become more punitive in their attempts to treat and prevent child abuse and neglect
    B. They have become more a means for identifying cases of abuse and less an agent for rehabilitation due to the large volume of cases
    C. They have become advocates for structured discipline within the school
    D. They have become a strong advocate in the court system

Answer: B. They have become more a means for identifying cases of abuse and less an agent for rehabilitation due to the large volume of cases
Child protective serves is the agency a teacher/school district would contact for suspected child abuse in a student.

83. **What is a benefit of frequent self-assessment?**
    (Average)

    A. Opens new venues for professional development
    B. Saves teachers the pressure of being observed by others
    C. Reduces time spent on areas not needing attention
    D. Offers a model for students to adopt in self-improvement

Answer: A. Opens new venues for professional development
When a teacher is involved in the process of self-reflection and self-assessment, one of the common outcomes is that the teacher comes to identify areas of skill or knowledge that require more research or improvement on her part. She may become interested in overcoming a particular weakness in her performance or may decide to attend a workshop or consult with a mentor to learn more about a particular area of concern.

84. **Mrs. Graham has taken the time to reflect, completed observations, and asked for feedback about the interactions between her and her students from her principal. It is obvious by seeking this information out that Mrs. Graham understands which of the following?**
    (Rigorous)

    A. The importance of clear communication with the principal
    B. She needs to analyze her effectiveness of classroom interactions
    C. She is clearly communicating with the principal
    D. She cares about her students

Answer: B. She needs to analyze her effectiveness of classroom interactions
By utilizing reflection, observations, and feedback from peers or supervisors, teachers can help to build their own understanding of how they interact with students. In this way, they can better analyze their effectiveness at building appropriate relationships with students.

85. **Which of the following are ways a professional can assess his/her teaching strengths and weaknesses?**
(Rigorous)

A. Examining how many students were unable to understand a concept
B. Asking peers for suggestions or ideas
C. Self-evaluation/reflection of lessons taught
D. All of the above

Answer: D. All of the above
It is important for teachers to involve themselves in constant periods of reflection and self-reflection to ensure they are meeting the needs of the students.

86. **In successful inclusion of students with disabilities:**
(Average)

A. A variety of instructional arrangements are available
B. School personnel shift the responsibility for learning outcomes to the student
C. The physical facilities are used as they are
D. Regular classroom teachers have sole responsibility for evaluating student progress

Answer: A. A variety of instructional arrangements are available
Here are some support systems and activities that are in evidence where successful inclusion has occurred:

Attitudes and beliefs

- The regular teacher believes the student can succeed
- School personnel are committed to accepting responsibility for the learning outcomes of students with disabilities
- School personnel and the students in the class have been prepared to receive a student with disabilities

87. **Teachers may duplicate copies of informational materials provided that they meet the following requirement/s:**
   (Rigorous)

   A. Brevity
   B. Spontaneity
   C. Cumulative effect
   D. All of the above

Answer: D. All of the above
Copyright is a type of protection provided by the United States to an author's literary works which also includes dramatic, musical, artistic, and other intellectual works. The conscientious use of these requirements will protect teachers and students from accusations of educational copyright infringement.

88. **Which of the following is one of the greatest obstacles that new teachers face when first entering the profession?**
   (Rigorous)

   A. Dealing with behavioral issues in the classroom
   B. Monitoring daily student success
   C. Developing rapport with parents and caretakers
   D. Creating weekly lesson plans

Answer: A. Dealing with behavioral issues in the classroom
Dealing with behavioral problems is one of the major concerns that teachers in the classroom face today. Disruptive behavior results in lost curriculum time and creates a classroom environment that is not always conducive to learning. Teachers should be proactive in dealing with behavioral issues at the time of the occurrence.

89. **How can a teacher use a student's permanent record?**
   (Average)

   A. To develop a better understanding of the needs of the student
   B. To record all instances of student disruptive behavior
   C. To brainstorm ideas for discussing with parents at parent-teacher conferences
   D. To develop realistic expectations of the student's performance early in the year

Answer: A. To develop a better understanding of the needs of the student
The purpose of a student's permanent record is to give the teacher a better understanding of the student's educational history and provide her with relevant information to support the student's learning. Permanent records may not be used to arrive at preconceived judgments or to build a case against the student. Above all, the contents of a student's permanent record are confidential.

90. **To what does the validity of a test refer?**
    (Rigorous)

    A. Its consistency
    B. Its usefulness
    C. Its accuracy
    D. The degree of true scores it provide

Answer: B. Its usefulness
The *Joint Technical Standards for Educational and Psychological Testing* APA, AERA, NCME, 1985) states: "Validity is the most important consideration in test evaluation. The concept refers to the appropriateness, meaningfulness and usefulness of *the specific inferences made from test scores*. Test validation is the process of accumulating evidence to support such inferences. A variety of inferences may be made from scores produced by a given test, and there are many ways of accumulating evidence to support any particular inference. Validity, however, is a unitary concept. Although evidence may be accumulated in many ways, validity always refers to the degree to which that evidence supports the inferences that are made from test scores."

TExES
GENERALIST 4-8
111

LANGUAGE ARTS SAMPLE TEST

1. **If a student has a poor vocabulary the teacher should recommend that:**
(Rigorous)

   A. The student read newspapers, magazines, and books on a regular basis
   B. The student enroll in a Latin class
   C. The student write the words repeatedly after looking them up in the dictionary
   D. The student use a thesaurus to locate synonyms and incorporate them into his/her vocabulary

2. **The arrangement and relationship of words in sentences or sentence structure best describes**
(Rigorous)

   A. Style
   B. Discourse
   C. Thesis
   D. Syntax

3. **Which of the following is a formal reading assessment?**
(Rigorous)

   A. A standardized reading test
   B. A teacher-made reading test
   C. An interview
   D. A reading diary

4. **The literary device of personification is used in which example below?**
(Average)

   A. "Beg me no beggary by soul or parents, whining dog!"
   B. "Happiness sped through the halls cajoling as it went."
   C. "O wind thy horn, thou proud fellow."
   D. "And that one talent which is death to hide."

5. **Which teaching method would be the most effective for interesting underachievers in the required senior English class?**
(Rigorous)

   A. Assign use of glossary work and extensively footnoted excerpts of great works
   B. Have students take turns reading aloud the anthology selection
   C. Let students choose which readings they'll study and write about
   D. Use a chronologically arranged, traditional text, but assigning group work, panel presentations, and portfolio management

6. **Which definition is the best for defining diction?**
(Rigorous)

   A. The specific word choices of an author to create a particular mood or feeling in the reader
   B. Writing which explains something thoroughly
   C. The background, or exposition, for a short story or drama
   D. Word choices which help teach a truth or moral

7. **Which is <u>not</u> a true statement concerning an author's literary tone?**
(Rigorous)

   A. Tone is partly revealed through the selection of details
   B. Tone is the expression of the author's attitude towards his/her subject
   C. Tone in literature is usually satiric or angry
   D. Tone in literature corresponds to the tone of voice a speaker uses

8. **What were two major characteristics of the first American literature?**
(Rigorous)

   A. Vengefulness and arrogance
   B. Bellicosity and derision
   C. Oral delivery and reverence for the land
   D. Maudlin and self-pitying egocentricism

9. **An example of the subject of a tall tale is**
(Rigorous)

   A. John Henry
   B. Paul Bunyan
   C. George Washington
   D. Rip Van Winkle

10. **Which term best describes the form of the following poetic excerpt?**
(Rigorous)

    And more to lulle him in his slumber soft,
    A trickling streake from high rock
    tumbling downe,
    And ever-drizzling raine upon the loft.
    Mixt with a murmuring winde, much like a swowne
    No other noyse, nor peoples troubles cryes.
    As still we wont t'annoy the walle'd towne,
    Might there be heard: but careless Quiet lyes,
    Wrapt in eternall silence farre from enemyes.

    A. Ballad
    B. Elegy
    C. Spenserian stanza
    D. Octava rima

11. **Which sonnet form describes the following?** *(Rigorous)*

My galley charg'd with forgetfulness,
Through sharp seas, in winter night doth pass
'Tween rock and rock; and eke mine enemy, alas,
That is my lord steereth with cruelness.
And every oar a thought with readiness,
As though that death were light in such a case.
An endless wind doth tear the sail apace
Or forc'ed sighs and trusty fearfulness.
A rain of tears, a cloud of dark disdain,
Hath done the wearied cords great hinderance,
Wreathed with error and eke with ignorance.
The stars be hid that led me to this pain
Drowned is reason that should me consort,
And I remain despairing of the poet

A. Petrarchan or Italian sonnet
B. Shakespearian or Elizabethan sonnet
C. Romantic sonnet
D. Spenserian sonnet

12. **A figure of speech in which someone absent or something inhuman is addressed as though present and able to respond describes** *(Average)*

A. Personification
B. Synechdoche
C. Metonymy
D. Apostrophe

13. **The quality in a work of literature which evokes feelings of pity or compassion is called** *(Easy)*

A. Colloquy
B. Irony
C. Pathos
D. Paradox

14. **An extended metaphor which compares two very dissimilar things–one lofty, one lowly, is a definition of a/an** *(Average)*

A. Antithesis
B. Aphorism
C. Apostrophe
D. Conceit

15. **Which of the following is a complex sentence?**
(Easy)

A. Anna and Margaret read a total of fifty-four books during summer vacation.
B. The youngest boy on the team had the best earned run average which mystifies the coaching staff.
C. Earl decided to attend Princeton; his twin brother Roy, who aced the ASVAB test, will be going to Annapolis.
D. "Easy come, easy go," Marcia moaned.

16. **Middle and high school students are more receptive to studying grammar and syntax**
(Rigorous)

A. Through worksheets and end of lessons practices in textbooks
B. Through independent, homework assignment
C. Through analytical examination of the writings of famous authors
D. Through application to their own writing

17. **A punctuation mark indicating omission, interrupted thought, or an incomplete statement is a/an**
(Easy)

A. Ellipsis
B. Anachronism
C. Colloquy
D. Idiom

18. **Which of the following contains an error in possessive inflection?**
(Easy)

A. Doris's shawl
B. Mother's-in-law frown
C. Children's lunches
D. Ambassador's briefcase

19. **Wally groaned, "Why do I have to do an oral interpretation of "The Raven."**
(Average)

A. Groaned "Why... of 'The Raven'?"
B. Groaned "Why... of "The Raven"?
C. Groaned ", Why... of "The Raven?"
D. Groaned, "Why... of "The Raven."

20. Mr. Smith <u>respectfully submitted his resignation and</u> <u>had</u> a new job.
(Average)

A. Respectfully submitted his resignation and has
B. Respectfully submitted his resignation before accepting
C. Respectfully submitted his resignation because of
D. Respectfully submitted his resignation and had

21. There were <u>fewer pieces</u> of evidence presented during the second trial
(Average)

A. fewer peaces
B. less peaces
C. less pieces
D. fewer pieces

22. The teacher <u>implied</u> from our angry words that there was conflict <u>between you</u> <u>and me.</u>
(Easy)

A. Implied… between you and I.
B. Inferred… between you and I.
C. Inferred… between you and me.
D. Implied… between you and me.

23. Which of the following is not one of the four forms of discourse?
(Average)

A. Exposition
B. Description
C. Rhetoric
D. Persuasion

24. "Clean as a whistle or "Easy as falling off a log" are examples of
(Average)

A. Semantics
B. Parody
C. Irony
D. Clichés

25. What is the figure of speech present in line one below in which the dead body of Caesar is addressed as though he were still a living being?
(Average)

O, pardon me, though Bleeding piece of earth
That I am meek and gentle with
These butchers.

Marc Antony from *Julius Caesar*

A. Apostrophe
B. Allusion
C. Antithesis
D. Anachronism

26. **A sixth-grade science teacher has given her class a paper to read on the relationship between food and weight gain. The writing contains signal words such as "because," "consequently," "this is how," and "due to." This paper has which text structure?**
(Rigorous)

A. Cause & effect
B. Compare & contrast
C. Description
D. Sequencing

27. **A form or discourse which explains or informs is**
(Average)

A. Exposition
B. Narration
C. Persuasion
D. Description

28. **The following passage is written from which point of view?**
(Rigorous)

As she mused the pitiful vision of her mother's life laid its spell on the very quick of her being –that life of commonplace sacrifices closing in final craziness. She trembled as she heard again her mother's voice saying constantly with foolish insistence: Dearevaun Seraun! Dearevaun Seraun!*
* "The end of pleasure is pain!" (Gaelic)

A. First person, narrator
B. Second person, direct address
C. Third person, omniscient
D. First person, omniscient

29. **Which of the following should not be included in the opening paragraph of an informative essay?**
(Average)

A. Thesis sentence
B. Details and examples supporting the main idea
C. A broad general introduction to the topic
D. A style and tone that grabs the reader's attention

30. **Which of the following is not a technique of prewriting?**
(Average)

   A. Clustering
   B. Listing
   C. Brainstorming
   D. Proofreading

31. **Which of the following is not an approach to keep students ever conscious of the need to write for audience appeal?**
(Rigorous)

   A. Pairing students during the writing process
   B. Reading all rough drafts before the students write the final copies
   C. Having students compose stories or articles for publication in school literary magazines or newspaper
   D. Writing letters to friends or relatives

Answer Key

1.	A		17.	A
2.	D		18.	B
3.	A		19.	A
4.	C		20.	C
5.	C		21.	D
6.	A		22.	C
7.	C		23.	C
8.	D		24.	D
9.	B		25.	B
10.	D		26.	A
11.	A		27.	A
12.	D		28.	C
13.	C		29.	B
14.	D		30.	D
15.	B		31.	B
16.	D			

Rigor Table

Easy
13, 15, 17, 18, 22

Average
4, 12, 14, 19, 20, 21, 23, 24, 25, 27, 29, 30

Rigorous
1, 2, 3, 5, 6, 7, 8, 9, 10, 11, 16, 26, 28, 31

LANGUAGE ARTS SAMPLE TEST WITH RATIONALES

1. **If a student has a poor vocabulary the teacher should recommend that:**
   (Rigorous)

   A. The student read newspapers, magazines, and books on a regular basis
   B. The student enroll in a Latin class
   C. The student write the words repeatedly after looking them up in the dictionary
   D. The student use a thesaurus to locate synonyms and incorporate them into his/her vocabulary

Answer: A. The student read newspapers, magazines, and books on a regular basis
It is up to the teacher to help the student choose reading material, but the student must be able to choose where s/he will search for the reading pleasure indispensable for enriching vocabulary.

2. **The arrangement and relationship of words in sentences or sentence structure best describes**
   (Rigorous)

   A. Style
   B. Discourse
   C. Thesis
   D. Syntax

Answer: D. Syntax
Syntax is the grammatical structure of sentences.

3. **Which of the following is a formal reading assessment?**
   (Rigorous)

   A. A standardized reading test
   B. A teacher-made reading test
   C. An interview
   D. A reading diary

Answer: A. A standardized reading text
If assessment is standardized, it has to be objective, whereas B, C and D are all subjective assessments.

4. **The literary device of personification is used in which example below?**
(Average)

A. "Beg me no beggary by soul or parents, whining dog!"
B. "Happiness sped through the halls cajoling as it went."
C. "O wind thy horn, thou proud fellow."
D. "And that one talent which is death to hide."

Answer: C. "O wind thy horn, thou proud fellow."
Personification gives human characteristics to an inanimate object, such as wind in the sentence above.

5. **Which teaching method would be the most effective for interesting underachievers in the required senior English class?**
(Rigorous)

A. Assign use of glossary work and extensively footnoted excerpts of great works
B. Have students take turns reading aloud the anthology selection
C. Let students choose which readings they'll study and write about
D. Use a chronologically arranged, traditional text, but assigning group work, panel presentations, and portfolio management

Answer: C. Let students choose which readings they'll study and write about
It will encourage students to react honestly to literature. Students should take notes on what they're reading so they will be able to discuss the material. They should not only react to literature, but also experience it. Small-group work is a good way to encourage them. The other answers are not fit for junior-high or high school students. They should be encouraged, however, to read critics of works in order to understand criteria work.

6. **Which definition is the best for defining diction?**
(Rigorous)

A. The specific word choices of an author to create a particular mood or feeling in the reader
B. Writing which explains something thoroughly
C. The background, or exposition, for a short story or drama
D. Word choices which help teach a truth or moral

Answer: A. The specific word choices of an author to create a particular mood or feeling in the reader
Diction refers to an author's choice of words, expressions, and style to convey his/her meaning.

7.   **Which is not a true statement concerning an author's literary tone?**
     (Rigorous)

     A. Tone is partly revealed through the selection of details
     B. Tone is the expression of the author's attitude towards his/her subject
     C. Tone in literature is usually satiric or angry
     D. Tone in literature corresponds to the tone of voice a speaker uses

Answer: C. Tone in literature is usually satiric or angry
Tone in literature conveys a mood and can be as varied as the tone of voice of a speaker (see D), e.g., sad, nostalgic, whimsical, angry, formal, intimate, satirical, sentimental, etc.

8.   **What were two major characteristics of the first American literature?**
     (Rigorous)

     A. Vengefulness and arrogance
     B. Bellicosity and derision
     C. Oral delivery and reverence for the land
     D. Maudlin and self-pitying egocentricism

Answer: D. Maudlin and self-pitying egocentricism
This characteristic can be seen in Captain John Smith's work as well as William Bradford's, and Michael Wigglesworth's works.

9.   **An example of the subject of a tall tale is**
     (Rigorous)

     A. John Henry
     B. Paul Bunyan
     C. George Washington
     D. Rip Van Winkle

Answer: B. Paul Bunyan
A tall tale is a Folklore genre, originating on the American frontier, in which the physical attributes, capabilities, and exploits of characters are wildly exaggerated. This is the case of giant logger Paul Bunyan of the American Northwestern forests. James Stevens traced Paul Bunyan to a French Canadian logger named Paul Bunyon. He won a reputation as a great fighter in the Papineau Rebellion against England in 1837 and later became famous as the boss of a logging camp. Paul Bunyan's first appearance in print seems to be in an advertising pamphlet, *Paul Bunyan and His Big Blue Ox*, published by the Red River Company. It immediately became very popular and was reissued many times.

10. **Which term best describes the form of the following poetic excerpt?**
    (Rigorous)

> And more to lulle him in his
> slumber soft,
> A trickling streake from high rock
> tumbling downe,
> And ever-drizzling raine upon
> the loft.
> Mixt with a murmuring winde,
> much like a swowne
> No other noyse, nor peoples
> troubles cryes.
> As still we wont t'annoy the
> walle'd towne,
> Might there be heard: but
> careless Quiet lyes,
> Wrapt in eternall silence farre
> from enemyes.

   A. Ballad
   B. Elegy
   C. Spenserian stanza
   D. Octava rima

Answer: D. Octava rima
The Octava Rima is a specific eight-line stanza whose rhyme scheme is ababbcc.

11. **Which sonnet form describes the following?**
   (Rigorous)

   My galley charg'd with
   forgetfulness,
   Through sharp seas, in
   winter night doth pass
   'Tween rock and rock; and
   eke mine enemy, alas,
   That is my lord steereth with
   cruelness.
   And every oar a thought with
   readiness,
   As though that death were
   light in such a case.
   An endless wind doth tear
   the sail apace
   Or forc'ed sighs and trusty
   fearfulness.
   A rain of tears, a cloud of dark
   disdain,
   Hath done the wearied
   cords great hinderance,
   Wreathed with error and eke
   with ignorance.
   The stars be hid that led me
   to this pain
   Drowned is reason that
   should me consort,
   And I remain despairing
   of the poet

   A. Petrarchan or Italian sonnet
   B. Shakespearian or Elizabethan sonnet
   C. Romantic sonnet
   D. Spenserian sonnet

Answer: A. Petrarchan or Italian sonnet
The Petrarchan sonnet, also known as the Italian sonnet, is named after the Italian poet Petrarch (1304-74). It is divided into an octave rhyming *abbaabba* and a sestet normally rhyming *cdecde*.

12. **A figure of speech in which someone absent or something inhuman is addressed as though present and able to respond describes**
(Average)

A. Personification
B. Synechdoche
C. Metonymy
D. Apostrophe

Answer: D. Apostrophe
Apostrophe gives human reactions and thoughts to animals, things, and abstract ideas alike. This figure of speech is often present in allegory: for instance, the Giant Despair in John Bunyon's *Pilgrim's Progress.* Also, fables use personification to make animals able to speak.

13. **The quality in a work of literature which evokes feelings of pity or compassion is called**
(Easy)

A. Colloquy
B. Irony
C. Pathos
D. Paradox

Answer: C. Pathos
A very well known example of pathos is Desdemona's death in Othello, but there are many other examples of pathos.

14. **An extended metaphor which compares two very dissimilar things– one lofty, one lowly, is a definition of a/an**
(Average)

A. Antithesis
B. Aphorism
C. Apostrophe
D. Conceit

Answer: D. Conceit
A conceit is an unusually far-fetched metaphor in which an object, person, or situation is presented in a parallel and simpler analogue between two apparently very different things or feelings, one very sophisticated and one very ordinary, usually taken either from nature or a well known every day concept familiar to both reader and author alike. The conceit was first developed by Petrarch and spread to England in the sixteenth century.

15. **Which of the following is a complex sentence?**
(Easy)

    A. Anna and Margaret read a total of fifty-four books during summer vacation.
    B. The youngest boy on the team had the best earned run average which mystifies the coaching staff.
    C. Earl decided to attend Princeton; his twin brother Roy, who aced the ASVAB test, will be going to Annapolis.
    D. "Easy come, easy go," Marcia moaned.

Answer: B. The youngest boy on the team had the best earned run average which mystifies the coaching staff.
Here, the use of the relative pronoun "which", whose antecedent is "the best run average", introduces a clause that is dependent on the independent clause "The youngest boy on the team had the best run average". The idea expressed in the subordinate clause is subordinate to the one expressed in the independent clause.

16. **Middle and high school students are more receptive to studying grammar and syntax**
(Rigorous)

    A. Through worksheets and end of lessons practices in textbooks
    B. Through independent, homework assignment
    C. Through analytical examination of the writings of famous authors
    D. Through application to their own writing

Answer: D. Through application to their own writing
At this age, students learn grammatical concepts best through practical application in their own writing.

17. **A punctuation mark indicating omission, interrupted thought, or an incomplete statement is a/an**
(Easy)

    A. Ellipsis
    B. Anachronism
    C. Colloquy
    D. Idiom

Answer: A. Ellipsis
In an ellipsis, a word or words that would clarify the sentence's message are missing, yet it is still possible to understand them from the context.

18. **Which of the following contains an error in possessive inflection?**
(Easy)

    A. Doris's shawl
    B. Mother's-in-law frown
    C. Children's lunches
    D. Ambassador's briefcase

Answer: B. Mother's-in-law frown
Mother-in-Law is a compound common noun and the inflection should be at the end of the word, according to the rule.

19. **Wally <u>groaned, "Why</u> do I have to do an oral interpretation of "The Raven."**
(Average)

    A. Groaned "Why... of 'The Raven'?"
    B. Groaned "Why... of "The Raven"?
    C. Groaned ", Why... of "The Raven?"
    D. Groaned, "Why... of "The Raven."

Answer: A. Groaned "Why... of 'The Raven'?"
The question mark in a quotation that is an interrogation should be within the quotation marks. Also, when quoting a work of literature within another quotation, one should use single quotation marks ('...') for the title of this work, and they should close before the final quotation mark.

20. **Mr. Smith <u>respectfully submitted his resignation and</u> <u>had</u> a new job.**
(Average)

    A. Respectfully submitted his resignation and has
    B. Respectfully submitted his resignation before accepting
    C. Respectfully submitted his resignation because of
    D. Respectfully submitted his resignation and had

Answer: C. Respectfully submitted his resignation because of
Choice A eliminates any relationship of causality between submitting the resignation and having the new job. Choice B just changes the sentence and does not indicate the fact that Mr. Smith had a new job before submitting his resignation. Choice D means that Mr. Smith first submitted his resignation then got a new job.

21.   There were <u>fewer pieces</u> of evidence presented during the second
      trial
      (Average)

      A. fewer peaces
      B. less peaces
      C. less pieces
      D. fewer pieces

Answer: D. fewer pieces
"Less" is impossible in the plural, and "peace" is the opposite of war, not a "piece"
of evidence.

22.   The teacher <u>implied</u> from our angry words that there was conflict
      <u>between</u> <u>you and me.</u>
      (Easy)

      A. Implied… between you and I.
      B. Inferred… between you and I.
      C. Inferred… between you and me.
      D. Implied… between you and me.

Answer: C. Inferred….between you and me.
The difference between the verb "to imply" and the verb "to infer" is that implying
is directing an interpretation toward other people; to infer is to deduce an
interpretation from someone else's discourse. Moreover, "between you and I" is
grammatically incorrect: after a preposition here "and", a disjunctive pronoun
(me, you, him, her, us, you, them) is needed.

23.   Which of the following is not one of the four forms of discourse?
      (Average)

      A. Exposition
      B. Description
      C. Rhetoric
      D. Persuasion

Answer: C. Rhetoric
Exposition, description, and persuasion are styles of writing and ways of
influencing a reader or a listener. Rhetoric, on the other hand, is theoretical. It is
the theory of expressive and effective speech. Rhetorical figures are ornaments
of speech such as anaphora, antithesis, metaphor, etc.

24. **"Clean as a whistle or "Easy as falling off a log" are examples of**
(Average)

   A. Semantics
   B. Parody
   C. Irony
   D. Clichés

Answer: D. Clichés
A cliché is a phrase or expression that has become dull due to overuse.

25. **What is the figure of speech present in line one below in which the dead body of Caesar is addressed as though he were still a living being?**
(Average)

   O, pardon me, though Bleeding piece of earth
   That I am meek and gentle with
   These butchers.

          Marc Antony from *Julius Caesar*

   A. Apostrophe
   B. Allusion
   C. Antithesis
   D. Anachronism

Answer: B. Allusion
This rhetorical figure addresses personified things, absent people or gods. An antithesis is a contrast between two opposing viewpoints, ideas, or presentation of characters. An anachronism is the placing of an object or person out of its time with the time of the text. The best known example is the clock in Shakespeare's *Julius Caesar*.

26. **A sixth-grade science teacher has given her class a paper to read on the relationship between food and weight gain. The writing contains signal words such as "because," "consequently," "this is how," and "due to." This paper has which text structure?**
(Rigorous)

    A. Cause & effect
    B. Compare & contrast
    C. Description
    D. Sequencing

Answer: A. Cause & effect
Cause and effect is the relationship between two things when one thing makes something else happen. Writers use this text structure to show order, inform, speculate, and change behavior. This text structure uses the process of identifying potential causes of a problem or issue in an orderly way. It is often used to teach social studies and science concepts. It is characterized by signal words such as because, so, so that, if... then, consequently, thus, since, for, for this reason, as a result of, therefore, due to, this is how, nevertheless, and accordingly.

27. **A form or discourse which explains or informs is**
(Average)

    A. Exposition
    B. Narration
    C. Persuasion
    D. Description

Answer: A. Exposition
Exposition sets forth a systematic explanation of any subject. It can also introduce the characters of a literary work and their situations in the story.

28. **The following passage is written from which point of view?**
(Rigorous)

As she mused the pitiful vision of her mother's life laid its spell on the very quick of her being –that life of commonplace sacrifices closing in final craziness. She trembled as she heard again her mother's voice saying constantly with foolish insistence: Dearevaun Seraun! Dearevaun Seraun!* * "The end of pleasure is pain!" (Gaelic)

A. First person, narrator
B. Second person, direct address
C. Third person, omniscient
D. First person, omniscient

Answer: C. Third person, omniscient
The passage is clearly in the third person (the subject is "she"), and it is omniscient since it gives the characters' inner thoughts.

29. **Which of the following should not be included in the opening paragraph of an informative essay?**
(Average)

A. Thesis sentence
B. Details and examples supporting the main idea
C. A broad general introduction to the topic
D. A style and tone that grabs the reader's attention

Answer: B. Details and examples supporting the main idea
The introductory paragraph should introduce the topic, capture the reader's interest, state the thesis and prepare the reader for the main points in the essay. Details and examples, however, should be given in the second part of the essay, so as to help develop the thesis presented at the end of the introductory paragraph, following the inverted triangle method consisting of a broad general statement followed by some information, and then the thesis at the end of the paragraph.

30. **Which of the following is not a technique of prewriting?**
(Average)

A. Clustering
B. Listing
C. Brainstorming
D. Proofreading

Answer: D. Proofreading
Proofreading should be reserved for the final draft.

31. **Which of the following is not an approach to keep students ever conscious of the need to write for audience appeal?**
(Rigorous)

A. Pairing students during the writing process
B. Reading all rough drafts before the students write the final copies
C. Having students compose stories or articles for publication in school literary magazines or newspaper
D. Writing letters to friends or relatives

Answer: B. Reading all rough drafts before the students write the final copies
Reading all rough drafts will not encourage the students to take control of their text and might even inhibit their creativity. On the contrary, pairing students will foster their sense of responsibility, and having them compose stories for literary magazines will boost their self esteem as well as their organization skills. As far as writing letters is concerned, the work of authors such as Madame de Sevigne in the seventeenth century is a good example of epistolary literary work.

MATHEMATICS SAMPLE TEST

1. $\dfrac{2^{10}}{2^5} =$

   (Average)

   A. 2^2
   B. 2^5
   C. 2^{50}
   D. $2^{\frac{1}{2}}$

2. $\left(\dfrac{^-4}{9}\right) + \left(\dfrac{^-7}{10}\right) =$

   (Average)

   A. $\dfrac{23}{90}$

   B. $\dfrac{^-23}{90}$

   C. $\dfrac{103}{90}$

   D. $\dfrac{^-103}{90}$

3. $0.74 =$
   (Easy)

   A. $\dfrac{74}{100}$

   B. 7.4%

   C. $\dfrac{33}{50}$

   D. $\dfrac{74}{10}$

4. $(5.6) \times \left(^-0.11\right) =$
   (Average)

   A. $^-0.616$
   B. 0.616
   C. $^-6.110$
   D. 6.110

5. **An item that sells for $375 is put on sale at $120. What is the percent of decrease?**
   (Easy)

   A. 25%
   B. 28%
   C. 68%
   D. 34%

6. **Which denotes an irrational number?**
   (Easy)

   A. 4.2500000
   B. $\sqrt{16}$
   C. 0.25252525
   D. $\pi = 3.141592$

7. What is the greatest common factor of 16, 28, and 36?
   (Average)

   A. 2
   B. 4
   C. 8
   D. 16

8. Compute the surface area of the prism below.
   (Average)

   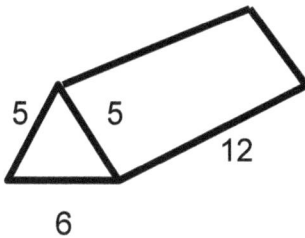

   A. 204
   B. 216
   C. 360
   D. 180

9. What is the area of a square whose side is 13 feet?
   (Easy)

   A. 169 feet
   B. 169 square feet
   C. 52 feet
   D. 52 square feet

10. The owner of a rectangular piece of land 40 yards in length and 30 yards in width wants to divide it into two parts. She plans to join two opposite corners with a fence as shown in the diagram below. The cost of the fence will be approximately $25 per linear foot. What is the estimated cost for the fence needed by the owner?
    (Rigorous)

    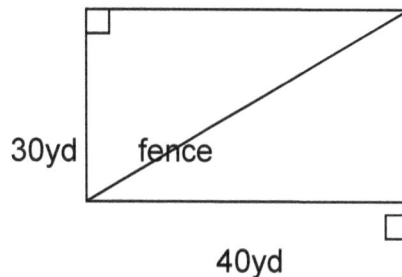

    A. $1,250
    B. $62,500
    C. $5,250
    D. $3,750

11. Find the surface area of a box which is 3 feet wide, 5 feet tall, and 4 feet deep.
    (Average)

    A. 47 sq. ft.
    B. 60 sq. ft.
    C. 94 sq. ft
    D. 188 sq. ft.

12. The trunk of a tree has a 2.1 meter radius. What is its circumference?
(Average)

   A. 2.1π square meters
   B. 4.2π meters
   C. 2.1π meters
   D. 4.2π square meters

13. Set A, B, C, and U are related as shown in the diagram. Which of the following is true, assuming not one of the six regions is empty?
(Average)

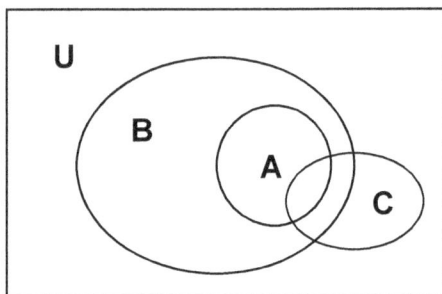

   A. Any element that is a member of set B is also a member of set A.
   B. No element is a member of all three sets A, B, and C.
   C. Any element that is a member of set U is also a member of set B.
   D. None of the above statements is true.

14. If $4x - (3 - x) = 7(x - 3) + 10$, then
(Rigorous)

   A. $x = 8$
   B. $x = -8$
   C. $x = 4$
   D. $x = -4$

15. It takes 5 equally skilled people 9 hours to shingle Mr. Joe's roof. Let t be the time required for only 3 of these men to do the same job. Select the correct statement of the given condition
(Rigorous)

   A. $\dfrac{3}{5} = \dfrac{9}{t}$

   B. $\dfrac{9}{5} = \dfrac{3}{t}$

   C. $\dfrac{5}{9} = \dfrac{3}{t}$

   D. $\dfrac{14}{9} = \dfrac{t}{5}$

16. Find the equation of a line through (5,6) and (-1,-2) in standard form.
(Rigorous)

   A. 3y=4x-2

   B. $-2y = \dfrac{4}{3}x - 1$

   C. 6y + 5x – 1

   D. y = 4x -6

17. **Find the real roots of the equation $3x^2 - 45 + 22x$.**
    (Rigorous)

    A. $\dfrac{^-5}{3}$ and 9

    B. $\dfrac{5}{3}$ and $^-9$

    C. 5 and 9

    D. -5 and -9

18. **{1,4,7,10, . . .} What is the 40th term in this sequence?**
    (Rigorous)

    A. 43
    B. 121
    C. 118
    D. 120

19. **Which term most accurately describes two coplanar lines without any common points?**
    (Average)

    A. Perpendicular
    B. Parallel
    C. Intersecting
    D. Skew

20. **Given similar polygons with corresponding sides 6 and 8, what is the area of the smaller polygon if the area of the larger polygon is 64?**
    (Rigorous)

    A. 48
    B. 36
    C. 144
    D. 78

21. **Study figures A, B, C, and D. Select the letter in which all triangles are similar.**
    (Easy)

    A.

    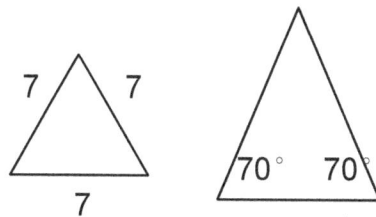

    B.

    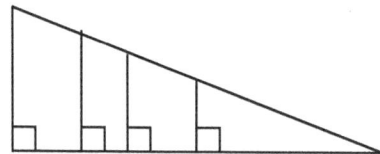

    C.

    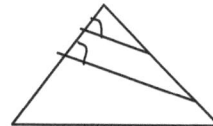

    D.

    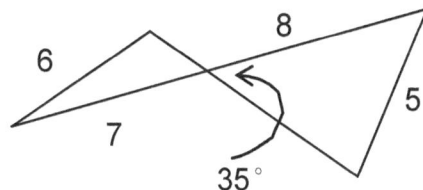

22. **Find the midpoint of (2,5) and (7,-4).**
    (Rigorous)

    A. (9,-1)
    B. (5, 9)
    C. (9/2, -1/2)
    D. (9/2, 1/2)

23. The following chart shows the yearly average number of international tourists visiting Palm Beach for 1990-1994. How many more international tourists visited Palm Beach in 1994 than in 1991?
(Average)

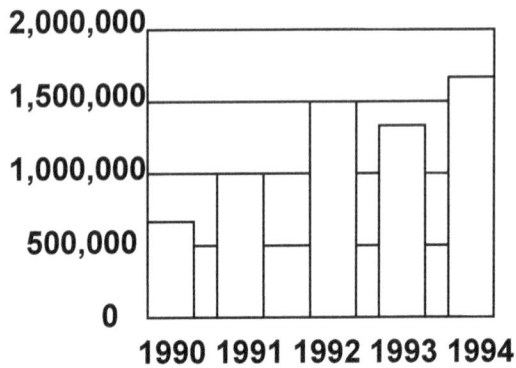

2,000,000
1,500,000
1,000,000
500,000
0

1990 1991 1992 1993 1994

A. 100,000
B. 600,000
C. 1,600,000
D. 8,000,000

24. What conclusion can be drawn from the graph below?
(Rigorous)

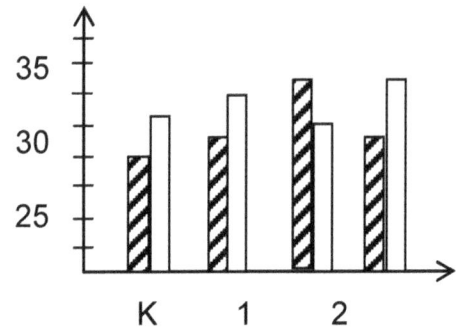

35
30
25

K   1   2

MLK Elementary
Student Enrollment   Girls   Boys

A. The number of students in first grade exceeds the number in second grade
B. There are more boys than girls in the entire school
C. There are more girls than boys in the first grade
D. Third grade has the largest number of students

25. Mary did comparison shopping on her favorite brand of coffee. Over half of the stores priced the coffee at $1.70. Most of the remaining stores priced the coffee at $1.80, except for a few who charged $1.90. Which of the following statements is true about the distribution of prices?
(Rigorous)

   A. The mean and the mode are the same
   B. The mean is greater than the mode
   C. The mean is less than the mode
   D. The mean is less than the median

26. What is the mode of the data in the following sample?
(Easy)

   9, 10, 11, 9, 10, 11, 9, 13

   A. 9
   B. 9.5
   C. 10
   D. 11

27. A coin is tossed and a die is rolled. What is the probability of landing on the head side of the coin and rolling a 3 on the dice?
(Rigorous)

   A. $\dfrac{1}{2}$

   B. $\dfrac{1}{6}$

   C. $\dfrac{1}{12}$

   D. $\dfrac{1}{15}$

28. What is the probability of drawing 2 consecutive aces from a standard deck of cards?
(Rigorous)

   A. $\dfrac{3}{51}$

   B. $\dfrac{1}{221}$

   C. $\dfrac{2}{104}$

   D. $\dfrac{2}{52}$

Answer Key

1. B
2. D
3. A
4. A
5. C
6. D
7. B
8. B
9. B
10. D
11. C
12. B
13. D
14. C
15. A
16. A
17. B
18. C
19. B
20. B
21. B
22. D
23. B
24. B
25. B
26. A
27. C
28. B

Rigor Table

Easy
3, 5, 6, 9, 21, 26

Average
1, 2, 4, 7, 8, 11, 12, 13, 19, 23

Rigorous
10, 14, 15, 16, 17, 18, 20, 22, 24, 25, 27, 28

MATHEMATICS SAMPLE TEST WITH RATIONALES

1. $\dfrac{2^{10}}{2^5} =$

   (Average)

   A. 2^2
   B. 2^5
   C. 2^{50}
   D. $2^{\frac{1}{2}}$

Answer: B. 2^5

The quotient rule of exponents says $\dfrac{a^m}{a^n} = a^{(m-n)}$ so $\dfrac{2^{10}}{2^5} = 2^{(10-5)} = 2^5$

2. $\left(\dfrac{^-4}{9}\right) + \left(\dfrac{^-7}{10}\right) =$

   (Average)

   A. $\dfrac{23}{90}$

   B. $\dfrac{^-23}{90}$

   C. $\dfrac{103}{90}$

   D. $\dfrac{^-103}{90}$

Answer: D. $\dfrac{^-103}{90}$

Find the LCD of $\dfrac{^-4}{9}$ and $\dfrac{^-7}{10}$. The LCD is 90, so you get $\dfrac{^-40}{90} + \dfrac{^-63}{90} = \dfrac{^-103}{90}$

3. **0.74 =**
   (Easy)

   A. $\dfrac{74}{100}$

   B. 7.4%

   C. $\dfrac{33}{50}$

   D. $\dfrac{74}{10}$

Answer: A. $\dfrac{74}{100}$

0.74⑧ the 4 is in the hundredths place, so the answer is $\dfrac{74}{100}$

4. $(5.6) \times (^-0.11) =$
   (Average)

   A. $^-0.616$
   B. 0.616
   C. $^-6.110$
   D. 6.110

Answer: A. $^-0.616$
Simply multiply 5.6 by -0.11. The answer will be negative because a positive times a negative is a negative number.

5. **An item that sells for $375 is put on sale at $120. What is the percent of decrease?**
   (Easy)

   A. 25%
   B. 28%
   C. 68%
   D. 34%

Answer: C. 68%
Use $(1 - x)$ as the discount. $375x = 120$.
$375(1 - x) = 120 \rightarrow 375 - 375x = 120 \rightarrow 375x = 255 \rightarrow x = 0.68 = 68\%$

6. **Which denotes an irrational number?**
    (Easy)

    A. 4.2500000
    B. $\sqrt{16}$
    C. 0.25252525
    D. π=3.141592

Answer: D. π=3.141592
An irrational number is neither terminal nor repeating. Rational numbers are either terminal or repeating. Of the choices given, only the value of pi (π) is an irrational number.

7. **What is the greatest common factor of 16, 28, and 36?**
    (Average)

    A. 2
    B. 4
    C. 8
    D. 16

Answer: B. 4
The smallest number in this set is 16; its factors are 1, 2, 4, 8 and 16. 16 is the largest factor, but it does not divide into 28 or 36. Neither does 8. 4 does factor into both 28 and 36.

8. **Compute the surface area of the prism below.**
   (Average)

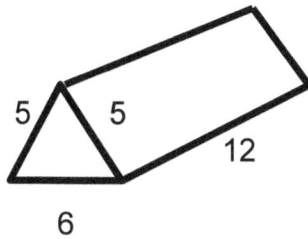

    A. 204
    B. 216
    C. 360
    D. 180

Answer: B. 216
There are five surfaces which make up the prism. The bottom rectangle has area 6 x 12 = 72. The sloping sides are two rectangles each with an area of 5 x 12 = 60. The height of the triangles is determined to be 4 using the Pythagorean Theorem. Therefore each triangle has area 1/2bh = 1/2(6)(4) =12. Thus, the surface area is 72 + 60 + 60 + 12 + 12 = 216.

9. **What is the area of a square whose side is 13 feet?**
   (Easy)

    A. 169 feet
    B. 169 square feet
    C. 52 feet
    D. 52 square feet

Answer: B. 169 square feet
Area = length times width (*lw*).
Length = 13 feet
Width = 13 feet (square, so length and width are the same).
Area = $13 \times 13 = 169$ square feet.
Area is measured in square feet.

10. The owner of a rectangular piece of land 40 yards in length and 30 yards in width wants to divide it into two parts. She plans to join two opposite corners with a fence as shown in the diagram below. The cost of the fence will be approximately $25 per linear foot. What is the estimated cost for the fence needed by the owner?
(Rigorous)

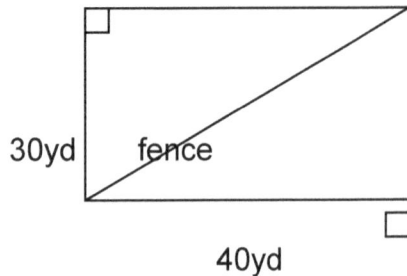

30yd | fence

40yd

A. $1,250
B. $62,500
C. $5,250
D. $3,750

Answer: D. $3,750
Find the length of the diagonal by using the Pythagorean Theorem. Let x be the length of the diagonal.

$$30^2 + 40^2 = x^2 \rightarrow 900 + 1600 = x^2$$
$$2500 = x^2 \rightarrow \sqrt{2500} = \sqrt{x^2}$$
$$x = 50 \text{ yards}$$

Convert to feet. $\dfrac{50 \text{ yards}}{x \text{ feet}} = \dfrac{1 \text{ yard}}{3 \text{ feet}} \rightarrow 150 \text{ feet}$

It cost $25.00 per linear foot, so the cost is (150 ft) ($25) = $3750

11. **Find the surface area of a box which is 3 feet wide, 5 feet tall, and 4 feet deep.**
(Average)

    A. 47 sq. ft.
    B. 60 sq. ft.
    C. 94 sq. ft
    D. 188 sq. ft.

Answer: C. 94 sq. ft.
Let's assume the base of the rectangular solid (box) is 3 by 4, and the height is 5. Then the surface area of the top and bottom together is 2(12) = 24. The sum of the areas of the front and back are 2(15) = 30, while the sum of the areas of the sides are 2(20)=40. The total surface area is therefore 94 square feet.

12. **The trunk of a tree has a 2.1 meter radius. What is its circumference?**
(Average)

    A. 2.1π square meters
    B. 4.2π meters
    C. $2.1\ \pi$ meters
    D. 4.2π square meters

Answer: B. 4.2π meters
Circumference is $2\pi r$, where r is the radius. The circumference is $2\pi 2.1 = 4.2\pi$ meters (not square meters because not measuring area).

13. **Set A, B, C, and U are related as shown in the diagram. Which of the following is true, assuming not one of the six regions is empty?**
(Average)

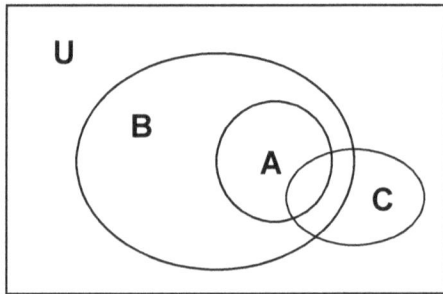

    A. Any element that is a member of set B is also a member of set A.
    B. No element is a member of all three sets A, B, and C.
    C. Any element that is a member of set U is also a member of set B.
    D. None of the above statements is true.

Answer: D. None of the above statements is true.
Answer A is incorrect because not all members of set B are also in set A. Answer B is incorrect because there are elements that are members of all three sets A, B, and C. Answer C is incorrect because not all members of set U is a member of set B. This leaves answer D, which states that none of the above choices are true.

14. **If $4x - (3 - x) = 7(x - 3) + 10$, then**
(Rigorous)

    A. $x = 8$
    B. $x = -8$
    C. $x = 4$
    D. $x = -4$

Answer: C. $x = 4$
The answer is **C.** Solve for x.
$$4x - (3 - x) = 7(x - 3) + 10$$
$$4x - 3 + x = 7x - 21 + 10$$
$$5x - 3 = 7x - 11$$
$$5x = 7x - 11 + 3$$
$$5x - 7x = {}^{-}8$$
$${}^{-}2x = {}^{-}8$$
$$x = 4$$

15. It takes 5 equally skilled people 9 hours to shingle Mr. Joe's roof. Let *t* be the time required for only 3 of these men to do the same job. Select the correct statement of the given condition
(Rigorous)

A. $\dfrac{3}{5} = \dfrac{9}{t}$

B. $\dfrac{9}{5} = \dfrac{3}{t}$

C. $\dfrac{5}{9} = \dfrac{3}{t}$

D. $\dfrac{14}{9} = \dfrac{t}{5}$

Answer: A . $\dfrac{3}{5} = \dfrac{9}{t}$

$$\dfrac{3 \text{ people}}{5 \text{ people}} = \dfrac{9 \text{ hours}}{t \text{ hours}}$$

16. **Find the equation of a line through (5,6) and (-1,-2) in standard form.**
(Rigorous)

A. 3y=4x-2

B. $-2y = \dfrac{4}{3}x - 1$

C. 6y + 5x – 1

D. y = 4x -6

Answer: A. 3y=4x-2

$$slope = \frac{y_2 - y_1}{x_2 - x_1} = \frac{-2-6}{^-1-5} = \frac{-8}{^-6} = \frac{4}{3}$$

$$Y - y_a = m(X - x_a) \rightarrow Y + 2 = \frac{4}{3}(X+1) \rightarrow$$

$$Y + 2 = \frac{4}{3}x + \frac{4}{3}$$

$$Y = \frac{4}{3}x - \frac{2}{3} \qquad \text{This is the slope-intercept form.}$$

Multiply by 3 to eliminate fractions

$$3y = 4x - 2 \qquad \text{This is the standard form.}$$

17. Find the real roots of the equation $3x^2 - 45 + 22x$.
(Rigorous)

A. $\dfrac{^-5}{3}$ and 9

B. $\dfrac{5}{3}$ and $^-9$

C. 5 and 9

D. -5 and -9

Answer: B. $\dfrac{5}{3}$ and $^-9$

Factor the equation $3x^2$ - 45 + 22x

(-)(+)

$(3x - 5)(x + 9)$ Set each part equal to 0 and solve for *x*.

$3x - 5 = 0$

$3x = 5$

$x = \dfrac{5}{3}$

$x + 9 = 0$

$x =^- 9$

18. {1,4,7,10, . . .} What is the 40th term in this sequence?
(Rigorous)

A. 43
B. 121
C. 118
D. 120

Answer: C. 118

To find a term in an arithmetic series in which each term is separated from the next by a fixed number, use the following formula: $a_n = a_1 + (n - 1)d$, where a_1 = the first term in the series, a_n = the nth term in the series, and d = the common difference between the terms.

a_n = 1 + (40 - 1)3
a_n = 1 + (39)3
a_n = 118

19. **Which term most accurately describes two coplanar lines without any common points?**
    (Average)

    A. Perpendicular
    B. Parallel
    C. Intersecting
    D. Skew

Answer: B. Parallel
By definition, parallel lines are coplanar lines without any common points.

20. **Given similar polygons with corresponding sides 6 and 8, what is the area of the smaller polygon if the area of the larger polygon is 64?**
    (Rigorous)

    A. 48
    B. 36
    C. 144
    D. 78

Answer: B. 36
In similar polygons, the areas are proportional to the squares of the sides. 36/64 = x/64.

21. **Study figures A, B, C, and D. Select the letter in which all triangles are similar.**
    (Easy)

A.

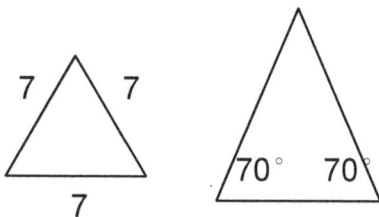

B.

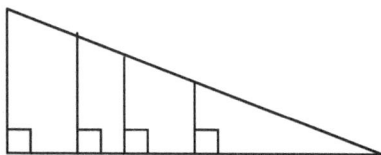

C.

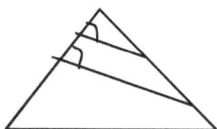

D.

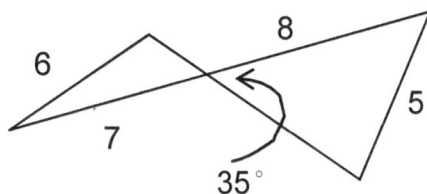

Answer: B.
Choice A is not correct because one triangle is equilateral and the other is isosceles. Choice C is not correct because the two smaller triangles are similar, but the large triangle is not. Choice D is not correct because the lengths and angles are not proportional to each other. Therefore, the correct answer is B because all the triangles have the same angles.

22. **Find the midpoint of (2,5) and (7,-4).**
    (Rigorous)

    A. (9,-1)
    B. (5, 9)
    C. (9/2, -1/2)
    D. (9/2, 1/2)

Answer: D. (9/2, 1/2)
Using the midpoint formula x = (2 + 7)/2   y = (5 + -4)/2

23. The following chart shows the yearly average number of international tourists visiting Palm Beach for 1990-1994. How many more international tourists visited Palm Beach in 1994 than in 1991? *(Average)*

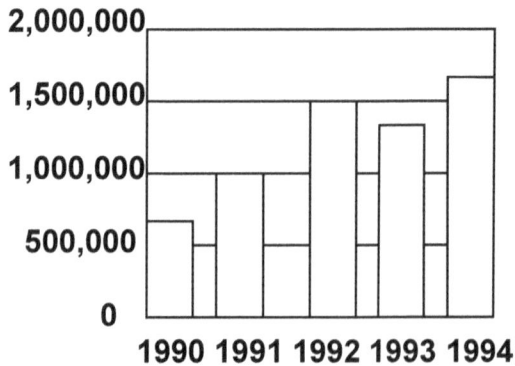

A. 100,000
B. 600,000
C. 1,600,000
D. 8,000,000

Answer: B. 600,000
The number of tourists in 1991 was 1,000,000 and the number in 1994 was 1,600,000. Subtract to get a difference of 600,000.

24. **What conclusion can be drawn from the graph below?**
(Rigorous)

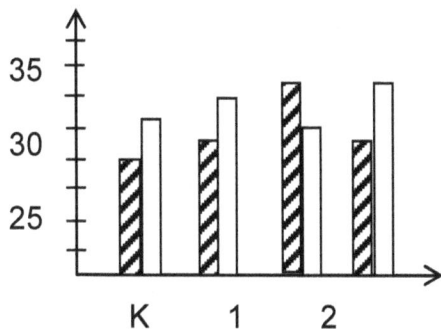

MLK Elementary
Student Enrollment   Girls   Boys

    A. The number of students in first grade exceeds the number in second grade
    B. There are more boys than girls in the entire school
    C. There are more girls than boys in the first grade
    D. Third grade has the largest number of students

Answer: B. There are more boys than girls in the entire school
In Kindergarten, first grade, and third grade, there are more boys than girls. The number of extra girls in grade two is more than made up for by the extra boys in all the other grades put together.

25. **Mary did comparison shopping on her favorite brand of coffee. Over half of the stores priced the coffee at $1.70. Most of the remaining stores priced the coffee at $1.80, except for a few who charged $1.90. Which of the following statements is true about the distribution of prices?**
(Rigorous)

    A. The mean and the mode are the same
    B. The mean is greater   than the mode
    C. The mean is less than the mode
    D. The mean is less than the median

Answer: B. The mean is greater than the mode
Over half the stores priced the coffee at $1.70, so this means that this is the mode. The mean would be slightly over $1.70 because other stores priced the coffee at over $1.70.

26. **What is the mode of the data in the following sample?**
    (Easy)

    9, 10, 11, 9, 10, 11, 9, 13

    A. 9
    B. 9.5
    C. 10
    D. 11

Answer: A. 9
The mode is the number that appears most frequently. Nine appears 3 times, which is more than the other numbers.

27. **A coin is tossed and a die is rolled. What is the probability of landing on the head side of the coin and rolling a 3 on the dice?**
    (Rigorous)

    A. $\dfrac{1}{2}$

    B. $\dfrac{1}{6}$

    C. $\dfrac{1}{12}$

    D. $\dfrac{1}{15}$

Answer: C. $\dfrac{1}{12}$

$P(\text{head}) = \dfrac{1}{2}. \quad P(3) = \dfrac{1}{6}$

$P(\text{head and 3}) = P(\text{head}) \times P(3)$
$$= \dfrac{1}{2} \times \dfrac{1}{6} = \dfrac{1}{12}$$

28. **What is the probability of drawing 2 consecutive aces from a standard deck of cards?**
(Rigorous)

A. $\dfrac{3}{51}$

B. $\dfrac{1}{221}$

C. $\dfrac{2}{104}$

D. $\dfrac{2}{52}$

Answer: B. $\dfrac{1}{221}$

There are 4 aces in the 52 card deck. P(first ace) = $\dfrac{4}{52}$. P(second ace) = $\dfrac{3}{51}$.

P(first ace and second ace) = P(one ace)xP(second ace|first ace) = $\dfrac{4}{52}$ x $\dfrac{3}{51}$ =

$\dfrac{1}{221}$.

SOCIAL SCIENCE SAMPLE TEST

1. The belief that the United States should control all of North America was called: *(Easy)*

    A. Westward expansion
    B. Pan Americanism
    C. Manifest Destiny
    D. Nationalism

2. The area of the United States was effectively doubled through purchase of the Louisiana Territory under which President? *(Average)*

    A. John Adams
    B. Thomas Jefferson
    C. James Madison
    D. James Monroe

3. A major quarrel between colonial Americans and the British concerned a series of British Acts of Parliament dealing with: *(Easy)*

    A. Taxes
    B. Slavery
    C. Native Americans
    D. Shipbuilding

4. The international organization established to work for world peace at the end of the Second World War is the: *(Average)*

    A. League of Nations
    B. United Federation of Nations
    C. United Nations
    D. United World League

5. Which famous battle fought on Texas soil resulted in Texas independence from Mexico? *(Rigorous)*

    A. The Battle of the Alamo
    B. The Battle of San Jacinto
    C. The Battle of the Rio Grande
    D. The Battle of Shiloh

6. **Why is the system of government in the United States referred to as a federal system?**
(Rigorous)

A. There are different levels of government
B. There is one central authority in which all governmental power is vested
C. The national government cannot operate except with the consent of the governed
D. Elections are held at stated periodic times, rather than as called by the head of the government

7. **The U.S. Constitution, adopted in 1789, provided for:**
(Rigorous)

A. Direct election of the President by all citizens
B. Direct election of the President by citizens meeting a standard of wealth
C. Indirect election of the President by electors
D. Indirect election of the President by the U.S. Senate

8. **From about 1870 to 1900 the settlement of America's "last frontier," the West, was completed. One attraction for settlers was free land, but it would have been to no avail without:**
(Rigorous)

A. Better farming methods and technology
B. Surveying to set boundaries
C. Immigrants and others to seek new land
D. The railroad to get them there

9. **Slavery arose in the Southern Colonies partly as a perceived economical way to:**
(Average)

A. Increase the owner's wealth through human beings used as a source of exchange
B. Cultivate large plantations of cotton, tobacco, rice, indigo, and other crops
C. Provide Africans with humanitarian aid, such as health care, Christianity, and literacy
D. Keep ships' holds full of cargo on two out of three legs of the "triangular trade" voyage.

10. The post-Civil War years were a time of low public morality, a time of greed, graft, and dishonesty. Which one of the reasons listed below would not be accurate reasons for this? *(Rigorous)*

   A. The war itself, because of the money and materials needed to conduct the War
   B. The very rapid growth of industry and big business after the War
   C. The personal example set by President Grant
   D. Unscrupulous heads of large impersonal corporations

11. A number of women worked hard in the first half of the 19th century for women's rights, but decisive gains did not come until after 1850. The earliest accomplishments were in: *(Average)*

   A. Medicine
   B. Education
   C. Writing
   D. Temperance

12. Of all the major causes of both World Wars I and II, the most significant one is considered to be: *(Average)*

   A. Extreme nationalism
   B. Military buildup and aggression
   C. Political unrest
   D. Agreements and alliances

13. Meridians, or lines of longitude, not only help in pinpointing locations but are also used for: *(Rigorous)*

   A. Measuring distance from the Poles
   B. Determining direction of ocean currents
   C. Determining the time around the world
   D. Measuring distance on the equator

14. The study of the ways in which different societies around the world deal with the problems of limited resources and unlimited needs and wants is in the area of: *(Average)*

   A. Economics
   B. Sociology
   C. Anthropology
   D. Political science

15. Capitalism and communism are alike in that they are both:
(Easy)

A. Organic systems
B. Political systems
C. Centrally planned systems
D. Economic systems

16. The purchase of goods or services on one market for immediate resale on another market is:
(Average)

A. Output
B. Enterprise
C. Arbitrage
D. Mercantile

17. The economic system promoting individual ownership of land, capital, and businesses with minimal governmental regulations is called:
(Easy)

A. Macro-economy
B. Micro-economy
C. Laissez-faire
D. Free enterprise

18. The American labor union movement started gaining new momentum:
(Rigorous)

A. During the building of the railroads
B. After 1865 with the growth of cities
C. With the rise of industrial giants such as Carnegie and Vanderbilt
D. During the war years of 1861-1865

19. It can be reasonably stated that the change in the United States from primarily an agricultural country into an industrial power was due to all of the following except:
(Average)

A. Tariffs on foreign imports
B. Millions of hardworking immigrants
C. An increase in technological developments
D. The change from steam to electricity for powering industrial machinery

20. There is no doubt of the vast improvement of the U.S. Constitution over the weak Articles of Confederation. Which one of the four accurate statements below is a unique yet eloquent description of the document?
(Rigorous)

A. The establishment of a strong central government in no way lessened or weakened the individual states
B. Individual rights were protected and secured
C. The Constitution is the best representation of the results of the American genius for compromise
D. Its flexibility and adaptation to change gives it a sense of timelessness

21. Marbury vs Madison (1803) was an important Supreme Court case which set the precedent for:
(Rigorous)

A. The elastic clause
B. Judicial review
C. The supreme law of the land
D. Popular sovereignty in the Territories

22. Which one of the following is not a function or responsibility of U.S. political parties?
(Rigorous)

A. Conducting elections or the voting process
B. Obtaining funds needed for election campaigns
C. Choosing candidates to run for public office
D. Making voters aware of issues and other public affairs information

23. Which of the following choices lists elements usually considered to be responsibilities of citizenship under the American system of government?
(Easy)

A. Serving in public office, voluntary government service, military duty
B. Paying taxes, jury duty, upholding the Constitution
C. Maintaining a job, giving to charity, turning in fugitives
D. Quartering of soldiers, bearing arms, government service

24. In which of the following disciplines would the study of physical mapping, modern or ancient, and the plotting of points and boundaries be least useful? *(Average)*

   A. Sociology
   B. Geography
   C. Archaeology
   D. History

25. The study of the exercise of power and political behavior in human society today would be conducted by experts in: *(Average)*

   A. History
   B. Sociology
   C. Political science
   D. Anthropology

Answer Key

1. C
2. B
3. A
4. C
5. B
6. A
7. C
8. D
9. B
10. C
11. B
12. A
13. C
14. A
15. D
16. C
17. D
18. B
19. A
20. C
21. B
22. A
23. B
24. A
25. C

Rigor Table

Easy
1, 3, 15, 17, 23

Average
2, 4, 9, 11, 12, 14, 16, 19, 24, 25

Rigorous
5, 6, 7, 8, 10, 13, 18, 20, 21, 22

SOCIAL SCIENCE SAMPLE TEST WITH RATIONALES

1. **The belief that the United States should control all of North America was called:**
   (Easy)

   A. Westward expansion
   B. Pan Americanism
   C. Manifest Destiny
   D. Nationalism

Answer: C. Manifest Destiny
The belief that the United States should control all of North America was called Manifest Destiny. This idea fueled much of the violence and aggression towards those already occupying the lands such as the Native Americans. Manifest Destiny was certainly driven by sentiments of nationalism, and gave rise to westward expansion.

2. **The area of the United States was effectively doubled through purchase of the Louisiana Territory under which President?**
   (Average)

   A. John Adams
   B. Thomas Jefferson
   C. James Madison
   D. James Monroe

Answer: B. Thomas Jefferson
The Louisiana Purchase, an acquisition of territory from France in 1803, occurred during the presidency of Thomas Jefferson. John Adams (1735-1826) was president from 1797–1801, before the purchase. James Madison (1751-1836) was president after the purchase (1809-1817). James Monroe (1758-1831) was actually a signatory on the Purchase, but did not become President until 1817.

3. **A major quarrel between colonial Americans and the British concerned a series of British Acts of Parliament dealing with:**
(Easy)

   A. Taxes
   B. Slavery
   C. Native Americans
   D. Shipbuilding

Answer: A. Taxes
Acts of Parliament imposing taxes on the colonists always provoked resentment. Because the colonies had no direct representation in Parliament, they felt it unjust that that body should impose taxes on them, with so little knowledge of their very different situation in America and no real concern for the consequences of such taxes. While slavery (B) continued to exist in the colonies long after it had been completely abolished in Britain, it never was a source of serious debate between Britain and the colonies. By the time Britain outlawed slavery in its colonies in 1833, the American Revolution had already occurred and the United States was free of British control. There was no series of British Acts of Parliament passed concerning Native Americans (C). Colonial shipbuilding (D) was an industry which received little interference from the British.

4. **The international organization established to work for world peace at the end of the Second World War is the:**
(Average)

   A. League of Nations
   B. United Federation of Nations
   C. United Nations
   D. United World League

Answer: C. United Nations
The international organization established to work for world peace at the end of the Second World War was the United Nations. From the ashes of the failed League of Nations, established following World War I, the United Nations continues to be a major player in world affairs today.

5. **Which famous battle fought on Texas soil resulted in Texas independence from Mexico?**
(Rigorous)

    A. The Battle of the Alamo
    B. The Battle of San Jacinto
    C. The Battle of the Rio Grande
    D. The Battle of Shiloh

Answer: B. The Battle of San Jacinto
It was the Battle of San Jacinto in which Sam Houston and the Texicans roundly defeated the Mexican army and captured Mexican General and Commander Santa Anna. The result was the independence of the Republic of Texas from Mexican control. The Battle of the Alamo (A), despite the defeat of the Texans by Santa Anna's troops, was a critical event which enabled Houston to gather troops and prepare for the Battle of San Jacinto. The Battle of Shiloh (D) occurred during the Civil War, and it was not in Texas. There was no major battle called the Battle of the Rio Grande (C).

6. **Why is the system of government in the United States referred to as a federal system?**
(Rigorous)

    A. There are different levels of government
    B. There is one central authority in which all governmental power is vested
    C. The national government cannot operate except with the consent of the governed
    D. Elections are held at stated periodic times, rather than as called by the head of the government

Answer: A. There are different levels of government
The United States is composed of fifty states, each responsible for its own affairs, but united under a federal government. A centralized system (B) is the opposite of a federal system. That national government cannot operate except with the consent of the governed (C) is a founding principle of American politics but is not a political system like federalism. A centralized democracy could still be consensual, but would not be federal. (D) is a description of electoral procedure, not a political system like federalism.

7.   **The U.S. Constitution, adopted in 1789, provided for:**
        (Rigorous)

        A. Direct election of the President by all citizens
        B. Direct election of the President by citizens meeting a standard of wealth
        C. Indirect election of the President by electors
        D. Indirect election of the President by the U.S. Senate

Answer: C. Indirect election of the President by electors
The United States Constitution has always arranged for the indirect election of the President by electors. The question, by mentioning the original date of adoption, might mislead someone to choose B, but while standards of citizenship have been changed by amendment, the President has never been directly elected. Nor does the Senate have anything to do with presidential elections. The House of Representatives, not the Senate, settles cases where neither candidate wins in the Electoral College.

8.   **From about 1870 to 1900 the settlement of America's "last frontier," the West, was completed. One attraction for settlers was free land, but it would have been to no avail without:**
        (Rigorous)

        A. Better farming methods and technology
        B. Surveying to set boundaries
        C. Immigrants and others to seek new land
        D. The railroad to get them there

Answer: D. The railroad to get them there
From about 1870 to 1900, the settlement of America's "last frontier" in the West was made possible by the building of the railroad. Without the railroad, the settlers never could have traveled such distances in an efficient manner.

9. **Slavery arose in the Southern Colonies partly as a perceived economical way to:**
   (Average)

   A. Increase the owner's wealth through human beings used as a source of exchange
   B. Cultivate large plantations of cotton, tobacco, rice, indigo, and other crops
   C. Provide Africans with humanitarian aid, such as health care, Christianity, and literacy
   D. Keep ships' holds full of cargo on two out of three legs of the "triangular trade" voyage.

Answer: B. Cultivate large plantations of cotton, tobacco, rice, indigo, and other crops

The Southern states, with their smaller populations, were heavily dependent on slave labor as a means of being able to fulfill their role and remain competitive in the greater U.S. economy. When slaves arrived in the South, the vast majority would become permanent fixtures on plantations, intended for work, not as a source of exchange. While some slave owners instructed their slaves in Christianity, provided health care or some level of education, such attention were not their primary reasons for owning slaves – a cheap and ready labor force was their reason. Whether or not ships' holds were full on two or three legs of the triangular journey was not the concern of Southerners as the final purchasers of slaves. Such details would have concerned the slave traders.

10. **The post-Civil War years were a time of low public morality, a time of greed, graft, and dishonesty. Which one of the reasons listed below would not be accurate reasons for this?**
(Rigorous)

A. The war itself, because of the money and materials needed to conduct the War
B. The very rapid growth of industry and big business after the War
C. The personal example set by President Grant
D. Unscrupulous heads of large impersonal corporations

Answer: C. The personal example set by President Grant

The post-Civil War years were a particularly difficult time for the nation, and public morale was especially low. The war had plunged the country into debt, and ultimately into a recession by the 1890s. Racism was rampant throughout the South and the North, where freed Blacks were taking jobs for low wages. The rapid growth of industry and big business caused a polarization of rich and poor, workers and owners. Many people moved into the urban centers to find work in the new industrial sector. These jobs typically paid low wages, required long hours, and offered poor working conditions. The heads of large impersonal corporations treated their workers inhumanely, letting morale drop to a record low. The heads of corporations tried to prevent and disband labor unions.

11. **A number of women worked hard in the first half of the 19th century for women's rights, but decisive gains did not come until after 1850. The earliest accomplishments were in:**
(Average)

A. Medicine
B. Education
C. Writing
D. Temperance

Answer: B. Education

Although women worked hard in the early nineteenth century to make gains in medicine, writing, and temperance movements, the most prestigious accomplishments of the early women's movement were in the field of education. Women such as May Wollstonecraft (1759-1797), Alice Palmer (1855-1902), and, of course, Elizabeth Blackwell (1821-1910) led the way for women, particularly in the area of higher education.

12. **Of all the major causes of both World Wars I and II, the most significant one is considered to be:**
(Average)

   A. Extreme nationalism
   B. Military buildup and aggression
   C. Political unrest
   D. Agreements and alliances

Answer: A. Extreme nationalism
Although military buildup and aggression, political unrest, and agreements and alliances were all characteristic of the world climate before and during World War I and World War II, the most significant cause of both wars was extreme nationalism. Nationalism is the idea that the interests and needs of a particular nation are of the utmost and primary importance above all else. Some nationalist movements could be liberation movements while others were oppressive regimes, much depends on their degree of nationalism.

The nationalism that sparked WWI included a rejection of German, Austro-Hungarian, and Ottoman imperialism by Serbs, Slavs and others culminating in the assassination of Archduke Ferdinand by a Serb nationalist in 1914. Following WWI and the Treaty of Versailles, many Germans and others in the Central Alliance Nations, malcontent at the concessions and reparations of the treaty, started a new form of nationalism. Adolf Hitler and the Nazi regime led this extreme nationalism. Hitler's ideas were examples of extreme, oppressive nationalism combined with political, social, and economic scapegoating and were the primary cause of WWII.

13. **Meridians, or lines of longitude, not only help in pinpointing locations but are also used for:**
(Rigorous)

   A. Measuring distance from the Poles
   B. Determining direction of ocean currents
   C. Determining the time around the world
   D. Measuring distance on the equator

Answer: C. Determining the time around the world
Meridians, or lines of longitude, are the determining factor in separating time zones and determining time around the world.

14. **The study of the ways in which different societies around the world deal with the problems of limited resources and unlimited needs and wants is in the area of:**
   (Average)

   A. Economics
   B. Sociology
   C. Anthropology
   D. Political science

Answer: A. Economics
The study of the ways in which different societies around the world deal with the problems of limited resources and unlimited needs and wants is a study of economics. Economists consider the law of supply and demand as fundamental to the study of the economy. However, sociology and political science also consider the study of economics and its importance in understanding social and political systems.

15. **Capitalism and communism are alike in that they are both:**
   (Easy)

   A. Organic systems
   B. Political systems
   C. Centrally planned systems
   D. Economic systems

Answer: D. Economic systems
While economic and political systems are often closely connected, capitalism and communism are primarily economic systems. Capitalism is a system of economics that allows the open market to determine the relative value of goods and services. Communism is an economic system where the market is planned by a central state. While communism is a centrally planned system, this is not true of capitalism. Organic systems (A) are studied in biology, a natural science.

16. **The purchase of goods or services on one market for immediate resale on another market is:**
   (Average)

   A. Output
   B. Enterprise
   C. Arbitrage
   D. Mercantile

Answer: C. Arbitrage
Output is an amount produced or manufactured by an industry. Enterprise is simply any business organization. Mercantile is one of the first systems of economics in which goods were exchanged. Arbitrage is an item or service that an industry produces. The dictionary definition of arbitrage is the purchase of securities on one market for immediate resale on another market in order to profit from a price discrepancy.

17. **The economic system promoting individual ownership of land, capital, and businesses with minimal governmental regulations is called:**
   (Easy)

   A. Macro-economy
   B. Micro-economy
   C. Laissez-faire
   D. Free enterprise

Answer: D. Free enterprise
Free enterprise or capitalism is the economic system that promotes private ownership of land, capital, and business with minimal government interference. Laissez-faire is the idea that an "invisible hand" will guide the free enterprise system to the maximum potential efficiency.

18. **The American labor union movement started gaining new momentum:**
     (Rigorous)

     A. During the building of the railroads
     B. After 1865 with the growth of cities
     C. With the rise of industrial giants such as Carnegie and Vanderbilt
     D. During the war years of 1861-1865

Answer: B. After 1865 with the growth of cities
The American Labor Union movement had been around since the late 18th and early 19th centuries. The Labor movement began to first experience persecution by employers in the early 1800s. The American Labor Movement remained relatively ineffective until after the Civil War. In 1866, the National Labor Union was formed, pushing such issues as the eight-hour workday and new policies of immigration. This gave rise to the Knights of Labor and eventually the American Federation of Labor (AFL) in the 1890s and the Industrial Workers of the World (1905). Therefore, it was the period following the Civil War that empowered the labor movement in terms of numbers, militancy, and effectiveness.

19. **It can be reasonably stated that the change in the United States from primarily an agricultural country into an industrial power was due to all of the following except:**
     (Average)

     A. Tariffs on foreign imports
     B. Millions of hardworking immigrants
     C. An increase in technological developments
     D. The change from steam to electricity for powering industrial machinery

Answer: A. Tariffs on foreign imports
It can be reasonably stated that the change in the United States from primarily an agricultural country into an industrial power was due to a great degree to three of the reasons listed above. It was a combination of millions of hard-working immigrants, an increase in technological developments, and the change from steam to electricity for powering industrial machinery. The only reason given that really had little effect was the tariffs on foreign imports.

20. **There is no doubt of the vast improvement of the U.S. Constitution over the weak Articles of Confederation. Which one of the four accurate statements below is a unique yet eloquent description of the document?**
(Rigorous)

    A. The establishment of a strong central government in no way lessened or weakened the individual states
    B. Individual rights were protected and secured
    C. The Constitution is the best representation of the results of the American genius for compromise
    D. Its flexibility and adaptation to change gives it a sense of timelessness

Answer: C. The Constitution is the best representation of the results of the American genius for compromise
The U.S. Constitution was indeed a vast improvement over the Articles of Confederation and the authors of the document took great care to assure longevity. It clearly stated that the establishment of a strong central government in no way lessened or weakened the individual states. In the Bill of Rights, citizens were assured that individual rights were protected and secured. Possibly the most important feature of the new Constitution was its flexibility and adaptation to change which assured longevity.

21. **Marbury vs Madison (1803) was an important Supreme Court case which set the precedent for:**
(Rigorous)

    A. The elastic clause
    B. Judicial review
    C. The supreme law of the land
    D. Popular sovereignty in the Territories

Answer: B. Judicial review
Marbury vs. Madison (1803) was an important case for the Supreme Court as it established judicial review. In that case, the Supreme Court set precedence to declare laws passed by Congress as unconstitutional.

22. **Which one of the following is not a function or responsibility of U.S. political parties?**
(Rigorous)

   A. Conducting elections or the voting process
   B. Obtaining funds needed for election campaigns
   C. Choosing candidates to run for public office
   D. Making voters aware of issues and other public affairs information

Answer: A. Conducting elections or the voting process
U.S. political parties have numerous functions and responsibilities. Among them are obtaining funds needed for election campaigns, choosing the candidates to run for office, and making voters aware of the issues. The political parties, however, do not conduct elections or the voting process, as that would be an obvious conflict of interest.

23. **Which of the following choices lists elements usually considered to be responsibilities of citizenship under the American system of government?**
(Easy)

   A. Serving in public office, voluntary government service, military duty
   B. Paying taxes, jury duty, upholding the Constitution
   C. Maintaining a job, giving to charity, turning in fugitives
   D. Quartering of soldiers, bearing arms, government service

Answer: B. Paying taxes, jury duty, upholding the Constitution
Only paying taxes, jury duty and upholding the Constitution are responsibilities of citizens as a result of rights and commitments outlined in the Constitution. For example, the right of citizens to a jury trial in the Sixth and Seventh Amendments and the right of the federal government to collect taxes in Article 1, Section 8. Serving in public office, voluntary government service and military duty, maintaining a job, giving to charity and turning in fugitives are all considered purely voluntary actions, even when officially recognized and compensated. The United States has none of the compulsory military or civil service requirements of many other countries. The quartering of soldiers is an act which, according to Amendment III of the Bill of Rights, requires a citizen's consent. Bearing arms is a right guaranteed under Amendment II of the Bill of Rights.

24. **In which of the following disciplines would the study of physical mapping, modern or ancient, and the plotting of points and boundaries be least useful?**
(Average)

   A. Sociology
   B. Geography
   C. Archaeology
   D. History

Answer: A. Sociology
In geography, archaeology, and history, the study of maps and plotting of points and boundaries is very important as all three of these disciplines hold value in understanding the spatial relations and regional characteristics of people and places. Sociology, however, mostly focuses on the social interactions of people and while location is important, the physical location is not as important as the social location such as the differences between studying people in groups or as individuals.

25. **The study of the exercise of power and political behavior in human society today would be conducted by experts in:**
(Average)

   A. History
   B. Sociology
   C. Political science
   D. Anthropology

Answer: C. Political science
Experts in the field of political science today would likely conduct the study of exercise of power and political behavior in human society. However, it is also reasonable to suggest that such studies would be important to historians (study of the past, often in an effort to understand the present), sociologists (often concerned with power structure in the social and political worlds), and even some anthropologists (study of culture and their behaviors).

SCIENCE SAMPLE TEST

1. **Chemicals should be stored**
    (Easy)

    A. In the principal's office
    B. In a dark room
    C. In an off-site research facility
    D. According to their reactivity with other substances

2. **When measuring the volume of water in a graduated cylinder, where does one read the measurement?**
    (Average)

    A. At the highest point of the liquid
    B. At the bottom of the meniscus curve
    C. At the closest mark to the top of the liquid
    D. At the top of the plastic safety ring

3. **When is a hypothesis formed?**
    (Easy)

    A. Before the data is taken
    B. After the data is taken
    C. After the data is analyzed
    D. Concurrent with graphing the data

4. **Which of the following is the most accurate definition of a non-renewable resource?**
    (Average)

    A. A nonrenewable resource is never replaced once used
    B. A nonrenewable resource is replaced on a timescale that is very long relative to human life-spans
    C. A nonrenewable resource is a resource that can only be manufactured by humans
    D. A nonrenewable resource is a species that has already become extinct

5. A scientist exposes mice to cigarette smoke, and notes that their lungs develop tumors. Mice that were not exposed to the smoke do not develop as many tumors. Which of the following conclusions may be drawn from these results?
(Rigorous)

I. Cigarette smoke causes lung tumors
II. Cigarette smoke exposure has a positive correlation with lung tumors in mice
III. Some mice are predisposed to develop lung tumors
IV. Cigarette smoke exposure has a positive correlation with lung tumors in humans

A. I and II only
B. II only
C. I , II, III and IV
D. II and IV only

6. Which of the following is a correct explanation for an astronaut's 'weightlessness'?
(Average)

A. Astronauts continue to feel the pull of gravity in space, but they are so far from planets that the force is small
B. Astronauts continue to feel the pull of gravity in space, but spacecraft have such powerful engines that those forces dominate, reducing effective weight
C. Astronauts do not feel the pull of gravity in space, because space is a vacuum
D. The cumulative gravitational forces, that the astronaut is experiencing, from all sources in the solar system equal out to a net gravitational force of zero

7. Physical properties are observable characteristics of a substance in its natural state. Which of the following are considered physical properties? *(Rigorous)*

   I   Color
   II Density
   III Specific gravity
   IV Melting point

   A. I only
   B. I and II only
   C. I, II, and III only
   D. III and IV only

8. The change in phase from liquid to gas is called: *(Rigorous)*

   A. Evaporation
   B. Condensation
   C. Vaporization
   D. Boiling

9. Which of the following statements is true of all transition elements? *(Rigorous)*

   A. They are all hard solids at room temperature
   B. They tend to form salts when reacted with Halogens
   C. They all have a silvery appearance in their pure state
   D. All of the above

10. A boulder sitting on the edge of a cliff has which type of energy? *(Easy)*

    A. Kinetic energy
    B. Latent energy
    C. No energy
    D. Potential energy

11. A converging lens produces a real image

    _____.

    (Rigorous)

    A. always
    B. never
    C. when the object is within one focal length of the lens
    D. when the object is further than one focal length from the lens

12. Which of the following is not a factor in how different materials will conduct seismic waves? *(Average)*

    A. Density
    B. Incompressiblity
    C. Rigidty
    D. Tensile strength

13. **The Law of Conservation of Energy states that:**
    (Average)

    A. There must be the same number of products and reactants in any chemical equation
    B. Mass and energy can be interchanged
    C. Energy is neither created nor destroyed, but may change form
    D. One form energy must remain intact (or conserved) in all reactions

14. **When you step out of the shower, the floor feels colder on your feet than the bathmat. Which of the following is the correct explanation for this phenomenon?**
    (Rigorous)

    A. The floor is colder than the bathmat
    B. The bathmat, being smaller than the floor, quickly reaches equilibrium with your body temperature
    C. Heat is conducted more easily into the floor
    D. Water is absorbed from your feet into the bathmat so it doesn't evaporate as quickly as it does off the floor, thus not cooling the bathmat as quickly

15. **Identify the correct sequence of organization of living things from lower to higher order:**
    (Average)

    A. Cell, organelle, organ, tissue, system, organism
    B. Cell, tissue, organ, organelle, system, organism
    C. Organelle, cell, tissue, organ, system, organism
    D. Organelle, tissue, cell, organ, system, organism

16. **Catalysts assist reactions by _____ .**
    (Easy)

    A. lowering required activation energy
    B. maintaining precise pH levels
    C. keeping systems at equilibrium
    D. changing the starting amounts of reactants

17. **Which process results in a haploid chromosome number?**
    (Rigorous)

    A. Mitosis
    B. Meiosis I
    C. Meiosis II
    D. Neither mitosis nor meiosis

18. A carrier of a genetic disorder is heterozygous for a disorder that is recessive in nature. Hemophilia is a sex-linked disorder. This means that: *(Easy)*

A. Only females can be carriers
B. Only males can be carriers
C. Both males and females can be carriers
D. Neither females nor males can be carriers

19. Which of the following is a correct explanation for scientific biological adaptation? *(Average)*

A. Giraffes need to reach higher for leaves to eat, so their necks stretch. The giraffe babies are then born with longer necks. Eventually, there are more long-necked giraffes in the population.
B. Giraffes with longer necks are able to reach more leaves, so they eat more and have more babies than other giraffes. Eventually, there are more long-necked giraffes in the population.
C. Giraffes want to reach higher for leaves to eat, so they release enzymes into their bloodstream, which in turn causes fetal development of longer-necked giraffes. Eventually, there are more long-necked giraffes in the population.
D. Giraffes with long necks are more attractive to other giraffes, so they get the best mating partners and have more babies. Eventually, there are more long-necked giraffes in the population.

20. An animal choosing its mate because of attractive plumage or a strong mating call is an example of: *(Average)*

   A. Sexual selection
   B. Natural selection
   C. Mechanical isolation
   D. Linkage

21. Many male birds sing long, complicated songs that describe thier identity and the area of land that they claim. Which of the answers below is the best decription of this behavior? *(Rigorous)*

   A. Innate territorial behavior
   B. Learned competitve behavior
   C. Innate mating behavior
   D. Learned territorial behavior

22. A wrasse (fish) cleans the teeth of other fish by eating away plaque. This is an example of _____ between the fish. *(Average)*

   A. parasitism
   B. symbiosis (mutualism)
   C. competition
   D. predation

23. Which of the following causes the aurora borealis? *(Rigorous)*

   A. Gases escaping from earth
   B. Particles from the sun
   C. Particles from the moon
   D. Electromagnetic discharges from the North pole

24. The transfer of heat from the earth's surface to the atmosphere is called: *(Average)*

   A. Convection
   B. Radiation
   C. Conduction
   D. Advection

25. **What is the most accurate description of the Water Cycle?**
(Rigorous)

A. Rain comes from clouds, filling the ocean. The water then evaporates and becomes clouds again.
B. Water circulates from rivers into groundwater and back, while water vapor circulates in the atmosphere.
C. Water is conserved except for chemical or nuclear reactions, and any drop of water could circulate through clouds, rain, ground-water, and surface-water.
D. Water flows toward the oceans, where it evaporates and forms clouds, which causes rain, which in turn flow back to the oceans after it falls.

26. **What makes up the largest abiotic portion of the Nitrogen Cycle?**
(Average)

A. Nitrogen fixing bacteria
B. Nitrates
C. Decomposers
D. Atomsphere

27. **What are the most significant and prevalent elements in the biosphere?**
(Easy)

A. Carbon, Hydrogen, Oxygen, Nitrogen, Phosphorus
B. Carbon, Hydrogen, Sodium, Iron, Calcium
C. Carbon, Oxygen, Sulfur, Manganese, Iron
D. Carbon, Hydrogen, Oxygen, Nickel, Sodium, Nitrogen

28. **Neap Tides are especially weak tides that occur when the Sun and Moon are in a perpendicular arrangment to the Earth, and Spring Tides are especially strong tides that occur when the Sun and Moon are in line. At which combination of lunar phases do these tides occur (respectively)?**
(Rigorous)

A. Half Moon and Full Moon
B. Quarter Moon and New Moon
C. Gibbous Moon and Quarter Moon
D. Full Moon and New Moon

29. **The planet with true retrograde rotation is:**
(Rigorous)

A. Pluto
B. Neptune
C. Venus
D. Saturn

30. **The phases of the Moon are the result of its _____ in relation to the Sun.**
(Average)

A. revolution
B. rotation
C. position
D. inclination

31. **The end of a geologic era is most often characterized by:**
(Average)

A. A general uplifting of the crust
B. The extinction of the dominant plants and animals
C. The appearance of new life forms
D. All of the above

32. **The best preserved animal remains have been discovered in:**
(Rigorous)

A. Resin
B. Fossil mold
C. Tar pits
D. Glacial ice

33. **Which type of student activity is most likely to expose a student's misconceptions about science?**
(Average)

A. Multiple-choice and fill-in-the-blank worksheets
B. Laboratory activities, where the lab is laid out step-by-step with no active thought on the part of the student
C. Teacher-lead demonstrations
D. Laboratories in which the students are forced to critically consider the steps taken and the results obtained

34. **In an experiment measuring the inhibition effect of different antibiotic discs of bacteria grown in Petri dishes, what are the independent and dependent variables respectively?**
(Rigorous)

A. Number of bacterial colonies and the antibiotic type
B. Antibiotic type and the distance between antibiotic and the closest colony
C. Antibiotic type and the number of bacterial colonies
D. Presence of bacterial colonies and the antibiotic type

Answer Key

1.	D		18.	A
2.	B		19.	B
3.	A		20.	A
4.	B		21.	D
5.	B		22.	B
6.	A		23.	B
7.	C		24.	C
8.	A		25.	C
9.	B		26.	D
10.	D		27.	A
11.	D		28.	B
12.	D		29.	C
13.	C		30.	C
14.	C		31.	D
15.	C		32.	C
16.	A		33.	D
17.	C		34.	B

Rigor Table

Easy
1, 3, 10, 16, 18, 27

Average
2, 4, 6, 12, 13, 15, 19, 20, 22, 24, 26, 30, 31, 33

Rigorous
5, 7, 8, 9, 11, 14, 17, 21, 23, 25, 28, 29, 32, 34

SCIENCE SAMPLE TEST WITH RATIONALES

1.   **Chemicals should be stored**
    (Easy)

    A. In the principal's office
    B. In a dark room
    C. In an off-site research facility
    D. According to their reactivity with other substances

Answer: D. According to their reactivity with other substances
Chemicals should be stored with other chemicals of similar properties (e.g., acids with other acids), to reduce the potential for either hazardous reactions in the store-room, or mistakes in reagent use. Certainly, chemicals should not be stored in anyone's office, and the light intensity of the room is not very important because light-sensitive chemicals are usually stored in dark containers. In fact, good lighting is desirable in a store-room, so that labels can be read easily. Chemicals may be stored off-site, but that makes their use inconvenient.

2.   **When measuring the volume of water in a graduated cylinder, where does one read the measurement?**
    (Average)

    A. At the highest point of the liquid
    B. At the bottom of the meniscus curve
    C. At the closest mark to the top of the liquid
    D. At the top of the plastic safety ring

Answer: B. At the bottom of the meniscus curve
To measure water in glass, you must look at the top surface at eye-level, and ascertain the location of the bottom of the meniscus (the curved surface at the top of the water). The meniscus forms because water molecules adhere to the sides of the glass, which is a slightly stronger force than their cohesion to each other. This leads to a U-shaped top of the liquid column, the bottom of which gives the most accurate volume measurement. (Other liquids have different forces, e.g., mercury in glass, which has a convex meniscus.)

3. **When is a hypothesis formed?**
   (Easy)

   A. Before the data is taken
   B. After the data is taken
   C. After the data is analyzed
   D. Concurrent with graphing the data

Answer: A. Before the data is taken
A hypothesis is an educated guess, made before undertaking an experiment. The hypothesis is then evaluated based on the observed data. Therefore, the hypothesis must be formed before the data is taken, not during or after the experiment.

4. **Which of the following is the most accurate definition of a non-renewable resource?**
   (Average)

   A. A nonrenewable resource is never replaced once used
   B. A nonrenewable resource is replaced on a timescale that is very long relative to human life-spans
   C. A nonrenewable resource is a resource that can only be manufactured by humans
   D. A nonrenewable resource is a species that has already become extinct

Answer: B. A nonrenewable resource is replaced on a timescale that is very long relative to human life-spans
Renewable resources are those that are renewed, or replaced, in time for humans to use more of them. Examples include fast-growing plants, animals, or oxygen gas. (Note that while sunlight is often considered a renewable resource, it is actually a nonrenewable but extremely abundant resource.) Nonrenewable resources are those that renew themselves only on very long timescales, usually geologic timescales. Examples include minerals, metals, or fossil fuels.

5.   A scientist exposes mice to cigarette smoke, and notes that their lungs develop tumors. Mice that were not exposed to the smoke do not develop as many tumors. Which of the following conclusions may be drawn from these results?
(Rigorous)

I.   Cigarette smoke causes lung tumors
II.   Cigarette smoke exposure has a positive correlation with lung tumors in mice
III. Some mice are predisposed to develop lung tumors
IV.   Cigarette smoke exposure has a positive correlation with lung tumors in humans

A. I and II only
B. II only
C. I , II, III and IV
D. II and IV only

Answer: B. II only
Although cigarette smoke has been found to cause lung tumors (and many other problems), this particular experiment shows only that there is a positive correlation between smoke exposure and tumor development in these mice. It may be true that some mice are more likely to develop tumors than others, which is why a control group of identical mice should have been used for comparison. Mice are often used to model human reactions, but this is as much due to their low financial and emotional cost as it is due to their being a "good model" for humans, and thus this scientist cannot make the conclusion that cigarette smoke exposure has a positive correlation with lung tumors in humans based on this data alone.

6. **Which of the following is a correct explanation for an astronaut's 'weightlessness'?**
    (Average)

    A. Astronauts continue to feel the pull of gravity in space, but they are so far from planets that the force is small
    B. Astronauts continue to feel the pull of gravity in space, but spacecraft have such powerful engines that those forces dominate, reducing effective weight
    C. Astronauts do not feel the pull of gravity in space, because space is a vacuum
    D. The cumulative gravitational forces, that the astronaut is experiencing, from all sources in the solar system equal out to a net gravitational force of zero

Answer: A. Astronauts continue to feel the pull of gravity in space, but they are so far from planets that the force is small
Gravity acts over tremendous distances in space (theoretically, infinite distance, though certainly at least as far as any astronaut has traveled). However, gravitational force is inversely proportional to distance squared from a massive body. This means that when an astronaut is in space, s/he is far enough from the center of mass of any planet that the gravitational force is very small, and s/he feels 'weightless'. Space is mostly empty (i.e., a vacuum), and spacecraft do have powerful engines. However, none of these has the effect attributed to it in the incorrect answer choices (B) or (C). Although, theoretically there is a point in space where the cumulative gravitational forces of sources within the solar system would equal a net force of zero, that point would be in constant motion and difficult to find, making answer D unlikely at best.

7. **Physical properties are observable characteristics of a substance in its natural state. Which of the following are considered physical properties?**
   (Rigorous)

   I   Color
   II Density
   III Specific gravity
   IV Melting point

   A. I only
   B. I and II only
   C. I, II, and III only
   D. III and IV only

Answer: C. I, II, and III only
Of the possibilities only the melting point of a substance cannot be found without altering the substance itself. Color is readily observable. Density can be measured without changing a substances form or structure, and specific gravity is a ratio based on density, so once one is known the other can be calculated. Thus answer (C) is the only possible answer.

8. **The change in phase from liquid to gas is called:**
   (Rigorous)

   A. Evaporation
   B. Condensation
   C. Vaporization
   D. Boiling

Answer: A. Evaporation
Condensation is the change in phase from a gas to a liquid. Vaporization is the conversion of matter to vapor - not all gases are vapors. Boiling is one method of inducing the change from a liquid to a gas; the process is called evaporation.

9. **Which of the following statements is true of all transition elements?**
   (Rigorous)

   A. They are all hard solids at room temperature
   B. They tend to form salts when reacted with Halogens
   C. They all have a silvery appearance in their pure state
   D. All of the above

Answer: B. They tend to form salts when reacted with Halogens
Answer (A) is incorrect because of Mercury, which has a low melting point and is thus a liquid at room temperature. Answer (C) is incorrect because Copper and Gold do not have a silvery appearance in their natural states. Since answers (A) and (C) are not correct then answer (D) cannot be correct either. This leaves only answer (B).

10. **A boulder sitting on the edge of a cliff has which type of energy?**
    (Easy)

    A. Kinetic energy
    B. Latent energy
    C. No energy
    D. Potential energy

Answer: D. Potential energy
Answer (A) would be true if the boulder fell off the cliff and started falling. Answer (C) would be a difficult condition to find since it would mean that no outside forces where operating on an object, and gravity is difficult to avoid. Answer (B) might be a good description of answer (D) which is the correct energy. The boulder has potential energy is imparted from the force of gravity.

11. **A converging lens produces a real image _____.**
    (Rigorous)

    A. always
    B. never
    C. when the object is within one focal length of the lens
    D. when the object is further than one focal length from the lens

Answer: D. when the object is further than one focal length from the lens
A converging lens produces a real image whenever the object is far enough from the lens (outside one focal length) so that the rays of light from the object can hit the lens and be focused into a real image on the other side of the lens. When the object is closer than one focal length from the lens, rays of light do not converge on the other side; they diverge. This means that only a virtual image can be formed, i.e., the theoretical place where those diverging rays would have converged if they had originated behind the object.

12. **Which of the following is not a factor in how different materials will conduct seismic waves?**
(Average)

   A. Density
   B. Incompressiblity
   C. Rigidty
   D. Tensile strength

Answer: D. Tensile strength
Density affects the speed at which seismic waves travel through the material. Incompressibilty has to do with how quickly a material compresses and rebounds as the waves hit it. The more compressable a material (and thus the slower the rebound) the slower the wave travels trhough the material. Seismic waves create a shearing force as they travel through a material, rigidity is the measure of the material's resistance to that shearing force. Tensile strength measures how far something can be stretched before breaking. Since seismic waves compress materials and are not stretching them that makes answer (D) the correct answer.

13. **The Law of Conservation of Energy states that:**
(Average)

   A. There must be the same number of products and reactants in any chemical equation
   B. Mass and energy can be interchanged
   C. Energy is neither created nor destroyed, but may change form
   D. One form energy must remain intact (or conserved) in all reactions

Answer: C. Energy is neither created nor destroyed, but may change form
Answer (C) is a summary of the Law of Conservation of Energy (for non-nuclear reactions). In other words, energy can be transformed into various forms such as kinetic, potential, electric, or heat energy, but the total amount of energy remains constant. Answer (A) is untrue, as demonstrated by many synthesis and decomposition reactions. Answers (B) and (D) may be sensible, but they are not relevant in this case.

14. **When you step out of the shower, the floor feels colder on your feet than the bathmat. Which of the following is the correct explanation for this phenomenon?**
(Rigorous)

A. The floor is colder than the bathmat
B. The bathmat, being smaller than the floor, quickly reaches equilibrium with your body temperature
C. Heat is conducted more easily into the floor
D. Water is absorbed from your feet into the bathmat so it doesn't evaporate as quickly as it does off the floor, thus not cooling the bathmat as quickly

Answer: C. Heat is conducted more easily into the floor
When you step out of the shower and onto a surface, the surface is most likely at room temperature, regardless of its composition (eliminating answer (A)). The bathmat is likely a good insulator and is unlikely to reach equilibrium with your body temperature after a short exposure so answer (B) is incorrect. Although evaporation does have a cooling effect, in the short time it takes you to step from the bathmat to the floor, it is unlikely to have a significant effect on the floor temperature (eliminating answer (D)).

Your feet feel cold when heat is transferred from them to the surface, which happens more easily on a hard floor than a soft bathmat. This is because of differences in specific heat (the energy required to change temperature, which varies by material). Therefore, the answer must be (C), i.e., heat is conducted more easily into the floor from your feet.

15. **Identify the correct sequence of organization of living things from lower to higher order:**
(Average)

A. Cell, organelle, organ, tissue, system, organism
B. Cell, tissue, organ, organelle, system, organism
C. Organelle, cell, tissue, organ, system, organism
D. Organelle, tissue, cell, organ, system, organism

Answer: C. Organelle, cell, tissue, organ, system, organism
Organelles are parts of the cell; cells make up tissue, which makes up organs. Organs work together in systems (e.g., the respiratory system), and the organism is the living thing as a whole.

16. **Catalysts assist reactions by _____ .**
    (Easy)

    A. lowering required activation energy
    B. maintaining precise pH levels
    C. keeping systems at equilibrium
    D. changing the starting amounts of reactants

Answer: A. Lowering required activation energy
Chemical reactions can be enhanced or accelerated by catalysts, which are present both with reactants and with products. They induce the formation of activated complexes, thereby lowering the required activation energy—so that less energy is necessary for the reaction to begin. Catalysts may require a well maintained pH to operate effectively, however they do not do this themselves. A catalyst, by lowering activation energy, may change a reaction's equilibrium point however, it does not maintain a system at equilibrium. The starting level of reactants is controlled separately from the addition of the catalyst, and has no direct correlation. Thus the correct answer is (A).

17. **Which process results in a haploid chromosome number?**
    (Rigorous)

    A. Mitosis
    B. Meiosis I
    C. Meiosis II
    D. Neither mitosis nor meiosis

Answer: C. Meiosis II
Meiosis is the division of sex cells. The resulting chromosome number is half the number of parent cells, i.e., a haploid chromosome number. Meiosis I mirrors Mitosis, resulting in diploid cells. It is only during Meiosis II that the number of chromosomes is halved. Mitosis, however, is the division of other cells, in which the chromosome number is the same as the parent cell chromosome number. Therefore, the answer is (B).

18. **A carrier of a genetic disorder is heterozygous for a disorder that is recessive in nature. Hemophilia is a sex-linked disorder. This means that:**
(Easy)

A. Only females can be carriers
B. Only males can be carriers
C. Both males and females can be carriers
D. Neither females nor males can be carriers

Answer: A. Only females can be carriers
Sice Hemophilia is a sex-linked disorder, the gene only appears on the X chromosome, with no counterpart on the Y chromosome. Since males are XY, they cannot be heterozygous for the trait; whatever is on the single X chromosome will be expressed. Females being XX can be heterozygous.

Answer (C) would describe a genetic disorder that is recessive and expressed on one of the somatic chromosomes (not sex-linked). Answer (D) would describe a genetic disorder that is dominant and expressed on any of the chromosomes. An example of answer (C) is sickle cell anemia. An example of answer (D) is Achondroplasia (the most common type of short-limbed dwarfism), in fact for this condition people that are Homozygous dominant for the gene that creates the disorder usually have severe health problems if they live past infancy, so almost all individuals with this disorder are carriers.

19. **Which of the following is a correct explanation for scientific biological adaptation?**
    (Average)

    A. Giraffes need to reach higher for leaves to eat, so their necks stretch. The giraffe babies are then born with longer necks. Eventually, there are more long-necked giraffes in the population.
    B. Giraffes with longer necks are able to reach more leaves, so they eat more and have more babies than other giraffes. Eventually, there are more long-necked giraffes in the population.
    C. Giraffes want to reach higher for leaves to eat, so they release enzymes into their bloodstream, which in turn causes fetal development of longer-necked giraffes. Eventually, there are more long-necked giraffes in the population.
    D. Giraffes with long necks are more attractive to other giraffes, so they get the best mating partners and have more babies. Eventually, there are more long-necked giraffes in the population.

Answer: B. Giraffes with longer necks are able to reach more leaves, so they eat more and have more babies than other giraffes. Eventually, there are more long-necked giraffes in the population.
Although evolution is often misunderstood, it occurs via natural selection. Organisms with a life/reproductive advantage will produce more offspring. Over many generations, this changes the proportions of the population. In any case, it is impossible for a stretched neck (A) or a fervent desire (C) to result in a biologically mutated baby. Although there are traits that are naturally selected because of mate attractiveness and fitness (D), this is not the primary situation here, so answer (B) is the best choice.

20. **An animal choosing its mate because of attractive plumage or a strong mating call is an example of:**
    (Average)

    A. Sexual selection
    B. Natural selection
    C. Mechanical isolation
    D. Linkage

Answer: A. Sexual Selection
The coming together of genes determines the makeup of the gene pool. Sexual selection, the act of choosing a mate, allows animals to have some choice in the breeding of its offspring.

21. **Many male birds sing long, complicated songs that describe thier identity and the area of land that they claim. Which of the answers below is the best decription of this behavior?**
(Rigorous)

   A. Innate territorial behavior
   B. Learned competitve behavior
   C. Innate mating behavior
   D. Learned territorial behavior

Answer: D. Learned territorial behavior
Birds often learn their songs, through a combination of trial and error, and listening to the songs of other members of their species (in some cases other species; this is called mimicry). Thus answers (A) and (C) are not correct. Typically a male bird will use a short song to impress a mate, the longer song is territorial because it is trying to convey to other males both identity and the territory that it claims.

22. **A wrasse (fish) cleans the teeth of other fish by eating away plaque. This is an example of _____ between the fish.**
(Average)

   A. parasitism
   B. symbiosis (mutualism)
   C. competition
   D. predation

Answer: B. symbiosis (mutualism)
When both species benefit from their interaction in their habitat, this is called symbiosis, or mutualism. In this example, the wrasse benefits from having a source of food, and the other fish benefit by having healthier teeth. Note that parasitism is when one species benefits at the expense of the other; competition is when two species compete with one another for the same habitat or food, and predation is when one species feeds on another.

23. **Which of the following causes the aurora borealis?**
   (Rigorous)

   A. Gases escaping from earth
   B. Particles from the sun
   C. Particles from the moon
   D. Electromagnetic discharges from the North pole

Answer: B. Particles from the sun
Aurora Borealis is a phenomenon caused by particles escaping from the sun. The particles escaping from the sun include a mixture of gases, electrons and protons, and are sent out at as force that scientists call solar wind. Together, we have the Earth's magnetosphere and the solar wind squeezing the magnetosphere and charged particles everywhere in the field. When conditions are right, the build-up of pressure from the solar wind creates an electric voltage that pushes electrons into the ionosphere. Here they collide with gas atoms, causing them to release both light and more electrons.

24. **The transfer of heat from the earth's surface to the atmosphere is called:**
   (Average)

   A. Convection
   B. Radiation
   C. Conduction
   D. Advection

Answer: C. Conduction
Radiation is the process of warming through rays or waves of energy, such as the Sun's rays warming the earth. The Earth returns heat to the atmosphere through conduction. Conduction is the transfer of heat through matter, such that areas of greater heat move to areas of lesser heat in an attempt to balance temperature.

25. **What is the most accurate description of the Water Cycle?**
(Rigorous)

    A. Rain comes from clouds, filling the ocean. The water then evaporates and becomes clouds again.
    B. Water circulates from rivers into groundwater and back, while water vapor circulates in the atmosphere.
    C. Water is conserved except for chemical or nuclear reactions, and any drop of water could circulate through clouds, rain, ground-water, and surface-water.
    D. Water flows toward the oceans, where it evaporates and forms clouds, which causes rain, which in turn flow back to the oceans after it falls.

Answer: C. Water is conserved except for chemical or nuclear reactions, and any drop of water could circulate through clouds, rain, ground-water, and surface-water.
All natural chemical cycles, including the Water Cycle, depend on the principle of Conservation of Mass. Any drop of water may circulate through the hydrologic system, ending up in a cloud, as rain, or as surface or ground-water. Although answers (A), (B) and (D) describe parts of the water cycle, the most comprehensive and correct answer is (C).

26. **What makes up the largest abiotic portion of the Nitrogen Cycle?**
(Average)

    A. Nitrogen fixing bacteria
    B. Nitrates
    C. Decomposers
    D. Atomsphere

Answer: D. Atomsphere
Since answers (A) and (C) are both examples of living organisms, they are biotic components of the nitrogen cycle. Nitrates are one type of nitrogen compound, (making it abiotic) that can be found in soil and in living organisms, however it makes up a small portion of the avaible nitrogen. The atmosphere being 78% Nitrogen gas (an abiotic component) makes up the largest source available to the Nitrogen Cycle.

27. **What are the most significant and prevalent elements in the biosphere?**
(Easy)

   A. Carbon, Hydrogen, Oxygen, Nitrogen, Phosphorus
   B. Carbon, Hydrogen, Sodium, Iron, Calcium
   C. Carbon, Oxygen, Sulfur, Manganese, Iron
   D. Carbon, Hydrogen, Oxygen, Nickel, Sodium, Nitrogen

Answer: A. Carbon, Hydrogen, Oxygen, Nitrogen, Phosphorus
Organic matter (and life as we know it) is based on Carbon atoms, bonded to Hydrogen and Oxygen. Nitrogen and Phosphorus are the next most significant elements, followed by Sulfur and then trace nutrients such as Iron, Sodium, Calcium, and others. If you know that the formula for any carbohydrate contains Carbon, Hydrogen, and Oxygen, that will help you narrow the choices to (A) and (D) in any case.

28. **Neap Tides are especially weak tides that occur when the Sun and Moon are in a perpendicular arrangment to the Earth, and Spring Tides are especially strong tides that occur when the Sun and Moon are in line. At which combination of lunar phases do these tides occur (respectively)?**
(Rigorous)

   A. Half Moon and Full Moon
   B. Quarter Moon and New Moon
   C. Gibbous Moon and Quarter Moon
   D. Full Moon and New Moon

Answer: B. Quarter Moon and New Moon
Spring tides are especially strong tides that occur when the Earth, Sun and Moon are in line, allowing both the Sun and the Moon to exert gravitational force on the Earth and increase tidal bulge height. These tides occur during the full moon and the new moon.

Neap tides occur during quarter moons, when the sun is illuminating half of the Moon's surface (the term quarter is used to refer to the fact that the Moon has traveled 1/2 of it's way through its cycle, not the amount of the surface illuminated by the Sun).

29. **The planet with true retrograde rotation is:**
(Rigorous)

A. Pluto
B. Neptune
C. Venus
D. Saturn

Answer: C. Venus
Venus has an axial tilt of only 3 degrees and a very slow rotation. It spins in the direction opposite of its counterparts (who spin in the same direction as the Sun). Uranus is also tilted and orbits on its side. However, this is thought to be the consequence of an impact that left the previously prograde rotating planet tilted in such a manner.

30. **The phases of the Moon are the result of its _____ in relation to the Sun.**
(Average)

A. revolution
B. rotation
C. position
D. inclination

Answer: C. position
The Moon is visible in varying amounts during its orbit around the earth. One half of the Moon's surface is always illuminated by the Sun (appears bright), but the amount observed can vary from full Moon to none.

31. **The end of a geologic era is most often characterized by:**
(Average)

A. A general uplifting of the crust
B. The extinction of the dominant plants and animals
C. The appearance of new life forms
D. All of the above

Answer: D. All of the above
Any of these things can be used to characterize the end of a geologic era, and often a combination of factors are applied to determining the end of an era.

32. **The best preserved animal remains have been discovered in:**
     (Rigorous)

     A. Resin
     B. Fossil mold
     C. Tar pits
     D. Glacial ice

Answer: C. Tar pits
Tar pits provide a wealth of information when it comes to fossils. Tar pits are oozing areas of asphalt, which were so sticky as to trap animals. These animals, without a way out, would die of starvation or be preyed upon. Their bones would remain in the tar pits, and be covered by the continued oozing of asphalt. Because the asphalt deposits were continuously added to, the bones were not exposed to much weathering, and we have found some of the most complete and unchanged fossils from these areas, including mammoths and saber toothed cats.

33. **Which type of student activity is most likely to expose a student's misconceptions about science?**
     (Average)

     A. Multiple-choice and fill-in-the-blank worksheets
     B. Laboratory activities, where the lab is laid out step-by-step with no active thought on the part of the student
     C. Teacher- lead demonstrations
     D. Laboratories in which the students are forced to critically consider the steps taken and the results obtained

Answer: D. Laboratories in which the students are forced to critically consider the steps taken and the results obtained
Answer (A) is a typical retain and repeat exercise, where a student just needs to remember the answer and doesn't need to understand it. Answer (B) is often called a cookie cutter lab because everything fits into a specific plan. Students are often able to guess the right answer without understanding the process. Teacher-lead demonstrations can be interesting for the students, and may challenge a student's misconceptions but misconceptions are often firmly routed and will require critical thought and reflection to change. Answer (D) requires active mental participation on the part of the student and thus is most likely to alter their understanding. These types of labs are often refered to as guided discovery laboratories.

34. **In an experiment measuring the inhibition effect of different antibiotic discs of bacteria grown in Petri dishes, what are the independent and dependent variables respectively?**
(Rigorous)

A. Number of bacterial colonies and the antibiotic type
B. Antibiotic type and the distance between antibiotic and the closest colony
C. Antibiotic type and the number of bacterial colonies
D. Presence of bacterial colonies and the antibiotic type

Answer: B. Antibiotic type and the distance between antibiotic and the closest colony
To answer this question, recall that the independent variable in an experiment is the entity that is changed by the scientist, in order to observe the effects of the change on the dependent variable. In this experiment, the antibiotic used is purposely changed so it is the independent variable.

Answers (A) and (D) list antibiotic type as the dependent variable and thus cannot be the correct answer, leaving answers (B) and (C) as the only two viable choices. The best answer is (B), because it measures at what concentration of the antibiotic the bacteria are able to grow, (as you move from the source of the antibiotic, the concentration decreases).

SAMPLE ESSAYS: SCIENCE

1. Use your accumulated knowledge to discuss the components of biogeochemical cycles.

BEST RESPONSE

Essential elements are recycled through an ecosystem. At times, the element needs to be made available in a useable form. Cycles are dependent on plants, algae and bacteria to fix nutrients for use by animals. The four main cycles are: water, carbon, nitrogen, and phosphorous.

Two percent of all the water is fixed in ice or the bodies of organisms, rendering it unavailable. Available water includes surface water (lakes, ocean, and rivers) and ground water (aquifers, wells). The majority (96%) of all available water is from ground water. Water is recycled through the processes of evaporation and precipitation. The water present now is the water that has been here since our atmosphere was formed.

Ten percent of all available carbon in the air (in the form of carbon dioxide gas) is fixed by photosynthesis. Plants fix carbon in the form of glucose; animals eat the plants and are able to obtain the carbon necessary to sustain themselves. When animals release carbon dioxide through respiration, the cycle begins again as plants recycle the carbon through photosynthesis.

Eighty percent of the atmosphere is in the form of nitrogen gas. Nitrogen must be fixed and taken out of gaseous form to be incorporated into an organism. Only a few genera of bacteria have the correct enzymes to break the strong triple bond between nitrogen atoms. These special bacteria live within the roots of legumes (peas, beans, alfalfa) and add bacteria to the soil so it may be taken-up by the plant. Nitrogen is necessary in the building of amino acids and the nitrogenous bases of DNA.

Phosphorus exists as a mineral and is not found in the atmosphere. Fungi and plant roots have structures called mycorrhizae that are able to fix insoluble phosphates into useable phosphorus. Urine and decayed matter returns phosphorus to the earth where it can be fixed in the plant. Phosphorus is needed for the backbone of DNA and for the manufacture of ATP.

The four biogeochemical cycles are present concurrently. Water is continually recycled, and is utilized by organisms to sustain life. Carbon is also a necessary component for life. Both water and carbon can be found in the air and on the ground. Nitrogen and phosphorous are commonly found in the ground. Special organisms, called decomposers, help to make these elements available in the environment. Plants use the recycled materials for energy and when they are consumed, the cycle begins again.

BETTER RESPONSE

Essential elements are recycled through an ecosystem. Cycles are dependent on plants, algae and bacteria to make nutrients available for use by animals. The four main cycles are: water, carbon, nitrogen, and phosphorous. Water is typically available as surface water (large bodies of water) or ground water. Water is recycled through the states of gas, liquid (rain), and solid (ice or snow). Carbon is necessary for life as it is the basis for organic matter. It is a byproduct of photosynthesis and is found in the air as carbon dioxide gas. Nitrogen is the largest component of the atmosphere. It is also necessary for the creation of amino acids and the nitrogenous bases of DNA. Phosphorous is another elemental cycle. Phosphorous is found in the soil and is made available by decomposition. It is then converted for use in the manufacture of DNA and ATP.

BASIC RESPONSE

Elements are recycled through an ecosystem. This occurs through cycles. These important cycles are called biogeochemical cycles. The water cycle consists of water moving from bodies of water into the air and back again as precipitation. The carbon cycle includes all organisms, as mammals breathe out carbon dioxide and are made of carbon molecules. Nitrogen is an amino building block and is found in soil. As things are broken down phosphorous is added to the earth, enriching the soil.

2. Examine the components of a eukaryotic cell.

BEST RESPONSE

The cell is the basic unit of all living things. Eukaryotic cells are found in protists, fungi, plants, and animals. Eukaryotic cells are organized. They contain many organelles, which are membrane bound areas for specific functions. Their cytoplasm contains a cytoskeleton that provides a protein framework for the cell. The cytoplasm also supports the organelles and contains the ions and molecules necessary for cell function. The cytoplasm is contained by the plasma membrane. The plasma membrane allows molecules to pass in and out of the cell. The membrane can bud inward to engulf outside material in a process called endocytosis. Exocytosis is a secretory mechanism, the reverse of endocytosis.

Eukaryotes have a nucleus. The nucleus is the brain of the cell that contains all of the cell's genetic information. The genetic information is contained on chromosomes that consist of chromatin, which is a complex of DNA and proteins. The chromosomes are tightly coiled to conserve space while providing a large surface area. The nucleus is the site of transcription of the DNA into RNA. The nucleolus is where ribosomes are made. There is at least one of these dark-staining bodies inside the nucleus of most eukaryotes. The nuclear envelope is two membranes separated by a narrow space. The envelope contains many pores that let RNA out of the nucleus.

Ribosomes are the site for protein synthesis. They may be free floating in the cytoplasm or attached to the endoplasmic reticulum. There may be up to a half a million ribosomes in a cell, depending on how much protein is made by the cell.

The endoplasmic reticulum (ER) is folded and provides a large surface area. It is the "roadway" of the cell and allows for transport of materials through and out of the cell. There are two types of ER. Smooth endoplasmic reticulum contains no ribosomes on their surface. This is the site of lipid synthesis. Rough endoplasmic reticulum has ribosomes on its surfaces. They aid in the synthesis of proteins that are membrane bound or destined for secretion.

Many of the products made in the ER proceed on to the Golgi apparatus. The Golgi apparatus functions to sort, modify, and package molecules that are made in the other parts of the cell. These molecules are either sent out of the cell or to other organelles within the cell. The Golgi apparatus is a stacked structure to increase the surface area.

Lysosomes are found mainly in animal cells. These contain digestive enzymes that break down food, substances not needed, viruses, damaged cell components and eventually the cell itself. It is believed that lysomomes are responsible for the aging process.

Mitochondria are large organelles that are the site of cellular respiration, where ATP is made to supply energy to the cell. Muscle cells have many mitochondria because they use a great deal of energy. Mitochondria have their own DNA, RNA, and ribosomes and are capable of reproducing by binary fission if there is a greater demand for additional energy. Mitochondria have two membranes: a smooth outer membrane and a folded inner membrane. The folds inside the mitochondria are called cristae. They provide a large surface area for cellular respiration to occur.

Plastids are found only in photosynthetic organisms. They are similar to the mitochondria due to the double membrane structure. They also have their own DNA, RNA, and ribosomes and can reproduce if the need for the increased capture of sunlight becomes necessary. There are several types of plastids. Chloroplasts are the sight of photosynthesis. The stroma is the chloroplast's inner membrane space. The stoma encloses sacs called thylakoids that contain the photosynthetic pigment chlorophyll. The chlorophyll traps sunlight inside the thylakoid to generate ATP which is used in the stroma to produce carbohydrates and other products. The chromoplasts make and store yellow and orange pigments. They provide color to leaves, flowers, and fruits. The amyloplasts store starch and are used as a food reserve. They are abundant in roots like potatoes.

The Endosymbiotic Theory states that mitochondria and chloroplasts were once free living and possibly evolved from prokaryotic cells. At some point in our evolutionary history, they entered the eukaryotic cell and maintained a symbiotic relationship with the cell, with both the cell and organelle benefiting from the relationship. The fact that they both have their own DNA, RNA, ribosomes, and are capable of reproduction helps to confirm this theory.

Found in plant cells only, the cell wall is composed of cellulose and fibers. It is thick enough for support and protection, yet porous enough to allow water and dissolved substances to enter. Vacuoles are found mostly in plant cells. They hold stored food and pigments. Their large size allows them to fill with water in order to provide turgor pressure. Lack of turgor pressure causes a plant to wilt.

The cytoskeleton, found in both animal and plant cells, is composed of protein filaments attached to the plasma membrane and organelles. They provide a framework for the cell and aid in cell movement. They constantly change shape and move about. Three types of fibers make up the cytoskeleton:

1. Microtubules – the largest of the three, they make up cilia and flagella for locomotion. Some examples are sperm cells, cilia that line the fallopian tubes, and tracheal cilia. Centrioles are also composed of microtubules. They aid in cell division to form the spindle fibers that pull the cell apart into two new cells. Centrioles are not found in the cells of higher plants.

2. Intermediate filaments – intermediate in size, they are smaller than microtubules but larger than microfilaments. They help the cell to keep its shape.

3. Microfilaments – smallest of the three, they are made of actin and small amounts of myosin (like in muscle tissue). They function in cell movement like cytoplasmic streaming, endocytosis, and ameboid movement. This structure pinches the two cells apart after cell division, forming two new cells.

BETTER RESPONSE

The cell is the basic unit of all living things. Eukaryotic cells are found in protists, fungi, plants, and animals. Eukaryotic cells are organized. Their cytoplasm contains a cytoskeleton that provides a protein framework for the cell. The cytoplasm is contained by the plasma membrane. The plasma membrane allows molecules to pass in and out of the cell.

Eukaryotes have a nucleus. The nucleus is the brain of the cell that contains all of the cell's genetic information. The chromosomes house genetic information and are tightly coiled to conserve space while providing a large surface area. The nucleus is the site of transcription of the DNA into RNA. The nucleolus is where ribosomes are made.

Ribosomes are the site for protein synthesis. There may be up to a half a million ribosomes in a cell, depending on how much protein is made by the cell.

The endoplasmic reticulum (ER) is folded and provides a large surface area. It is the "roadway" of the cell and allows for transport of materials through and out of the cell. It may be smooth or rough.

Many of the products made in the ER proceed on to the Golgi apparatus. The Golgi apparatus functions to sort, modify, and package molecules that are made in the other parts of the cell.

Mitochondria are large organelles that are the site of cellular respiration, where ATP is made to supply energy to the cell. Mitochondria have their own DNA, RNA, and ribosomes and are capable of reproducing by binary fission if there is a greater demand for additional energy.

Plastids are found only in photosynthetic organisms. They are similar to the mitochondria. They also have their own DNA, RNA, and ribosomes and can reproduce if the need for the increased capture of sunlight becomes necessary.

Found in plant cells only, the cell wall is composed of cellulose and fibers. It is thick enough for support and protection, yet porous enough to allow water and dissolved substances to enter.

The cytoskeleton, found in both animal and plant cells, is composed of protein filaments attached to the plasma membrane and organelles. They provide a framework for the cell and aid in cell movement. They constantly change shape and move about. Three types of fibers make up the cytoskeleton (in order of size: largest-smallest): microtubules, intermediate filaments, microfilaments.

BASIC RESPONSE

The cell is the basic unit of all living things. Eukaryotic cells contain many organelles. Eukaryotes have a nucleus. The nucleus is the brain of the cell that contains all of the cell's genetic information. The nucleus is the site of DNA transcription. There is at least one nucleolus inside the nucleus of most eukaryotes. Ribosomes are the site for protein synthesis and can be found on the endoplasmic reticulum (ER). The Golgi apparatus functions to sort, modify, and package molecules that are made in the other parts of the cell. Mitochondria are large organelles that are the site of cellular respiration, where ATP is made to supply energy to the cell.

In plant cells, the cell wall is composed of cellulose and fibers. The cytoskeleton, found in both animal and plant cells, is composed of protein filaments. The three types of fibers differ in size and help the cell to keep its shape and aid in movement.

3. Discuss the scientific process.

BEST RESPONSE

Science may be defined as a body of knowledge that is systematically derived from study, observations, and experimentation. Its goal is to identify and establish principles and theories that may be applied to solve problems. Pseudoscience, on the other hand, is a belief that is not warranted. There is no scientific methodology or application. Some of the more classic examples of pseudoscience include witchcraft, alien encounters or any topic that is explained by hearsay.

Scientific theory and experimentation must be repeatable. It is also possible to be disproved and is capable of change. Science depends on communication, agreement, and disagreement among scientists. It is composed of theories, laws, and hypotheses.

> Theory - the formation of principles or relationships which have been verified and accepted.

> Law - an explanation of events that occur with uniformity under the same conditions (laws of nature, law of gravitation).

> Hypothesis - an unproved theory or educated guess followed by research to best explain a phenomena. A theory is a proven hypothesis.

Science is limited by the available technology. An example of this would be the relationship of the discovery of the cell and the invention of the microscope. As our technology improves, more hypotheses will become theories and possibly laws. Science is also limited by the data that is able to be collected. Data may be interpreted differently on different occasions. Science limitations cause explanations to be changeable as new technologies emerge.

The first step in scientific inquiry is posing a question to be answered. Next, a hypothesis is formed to provide a plausible explanation. An experiment is then proposed and performed to test this hypothesis. A comparison between the predicted and observed results is the next step. Conclusions are then formed and it is determined whether the hypothesis is correct or incorrect. If incorrect, the next step is to form a new hypothesis and the process is repeated.

BETTER RESPONSE

Science is derived from study, observations, and experimentation. Its goal is to identify and establish principles and theories that may be applied to solve problems. Scientific theory and experimentation must be repeatable. It is also possible to disprove or change a theory. Science depends on communication, agreement, and disagreement among scientists. It is composed of theories, laws, and hypotheses. A theory is a principle or relationship that has been verified and accepted through experiments. A law is an explanation of events that occur with uniformity under the same conditions. A hypothesis is an educated guess followed by research. A theory is a proven hypothesis.

Science is limited by the available technology. An example of this would be the relationship of the discovery of the cell and the invention of the microscope. The first step in scientific inquiry is posing a question to be answered. Next, a hypothesis is formed to provide a plausible explanation. An experiment is then proposed and performed to test this hypothesis. A comparison between the predicted and observed results is the next step. Conclusions are then formed and it is determined whether the hypothesis is correct or incorrect. If incorrect, the next step is to form a new hypothesis and the process is repeated.

BASIC RESPONSE

Science is composed of theories, laws, and hypotheses. The first step in scientific inquiry is posing a question to be answered. Next, a hypothesis is formed to provide a plausible explanation. An experiment is then proposed and performed to test this hypothesis. A comparison between the predicted and observed results is the next step. Conclusions are then formed and it is determined whether the hypothesis is correct or incorrect. If incorrect, the next step is to form a new hypothesis and the process is repeated. Science is always limited by the available technology.

www.ingramcontent.com/pod-product-compliance
Lightning Source LLC
Chambersburg PA
CBHW080458110426
42742CB00017B/2924

9 781607 873075